78 RPM RECORDS & PRICES

by

Peter A. Soderbergh, Ph.D.
Dean of the College of Education
Louisiana State University

Published by
WALLACE-HOMESTEAD BOOK COMPANY
P.O. Box BI
Des Moines, Iowa 50304

Contents

Acknowledgments

I owe much to the following professional dealers: Mr. N. E. Pierce of Jack's Record Cellar in San Francisco; Mr. T. M. Thibault of Cedar Brook, New Jersey, whose stock exceeds 300,000 records; Mr. John Sicignano of Nutley, New Jersey; Mr. Robert Nichols of Atlanta; Mr. Frederick Williams of Philadelphia; and "Mr. Records," Leon Kloppholz of Hillside, New Jersey. When I asked for information and/or opinion from them I was treated with courtesy. From their responses to questions about contemporary markets I have drawn much substance. I am indebted also to the editor of American Collector, who gave permission to use a large portion of my article in his May, 1975 issue as the basis for the introduction to this guide. Finally, on a different level, I want to express my retroactive gratitude to my late father, Sven E. Soderbergh, and to my mother, Mary M. Soderbergh. Had they not permitted me to purchase, and constantly listen to, my modest, noisy collection of 78's some 35 years ago this book most certainly would never have been written.

P.A.S.

Dedication

To my wife, Midge, and to the children . . .

Susan

Mary

Peter

Katherine

Steven

Charley

. . . who have endured me and my 78's all these years.

Introduction

Since 1970 a large segment of our population has been afflicted with TC (Terminal Collectibilitis). Americans, in ever-increasing numbers, are buying up, searching for, writing about, and dealing in old banks, bells, bottles, brass, buttons, cards, coins, comics, dolls, glass, marbles, mugs, stereopticons—and scores of other objects they disdained (or discarded) previously. As Ralph and Terry Kovel noted in their *Complete Antiques Price List* several years back: "The nostalgia craze is continuing, and the everyday items that would have been ignored a few years ago are now bringing good money."

T.C., in its most virulent phase, is highly contagious. And it strikes without any real warning. One casual visit to a local garage sale or a drive-in flea market; one innocent swing through an "antique" store; one unplanned stopover at an auction—especially if the victim comes away with something he or she has "always wanted" for 50 cents—and another citizen is infected. He then passes his raging virus to his friends, whom he lures to the "Old Curiosity Shoppe" the very next weekend, and so on. Carriers are everywhere. There is no known cure. Fortunately this national ailment is not fatal. It causes people to divorce, build extra rooms to hold their collectibles, and go bankrupt—but no one has died from T.C. to date.

One clear symptom of T.C. is evident when people who are apparently normal on Saturday suddenly begin to rummage madly through closets, storage trunks, and garages on Monday. T.C. knows no social class. It strikes rich and poor alike. It is a very democratic disease.

In recent years those who pilfer basements and attics have been discovering 78 rpm records. They pause, and wonder: Are these records worth anything?

Everything else seems to be selling—why not my old records? Do I have a goldmine right here in my own home? Nostrils flare and fevers rise.

It is natural to believe that those heavy, red-label Carusos, Glucks, and Schumann-Heinks are priceless. It is human to hope that the rediscovered Millers, Dorseys, and Goodmans are invaluable. It is tempting to contemplate how much that mildewed album of "rare" discs will inflate the bank balance (or your grandchildren's estate). Visions of a vast marketplace crowded with prospective buyers flash across your stricken brain as you glance down at those black discs with renewed appreciation.

Is it all a dream, or a hallucination induced by the current epidemic? Well, it is significant that in his fine book *Collecting Nostalgia* (1972), a 367-page study of Nouveaux Junque, John Mebane devotes only three sentences to the old phonograph records. The Kovels' compendium has over 40,000 entries. Just 37 are listed under "Music, Record," and 20 of those are Edison cylinders. That's not too encouraging. But then, hope springs eternal. Perhaps you *are* sitting (ever so lightly) on a stack of dusty, 10-inch nuggets. What to do? Whom to tell? How to act.

Before worrying too much about the value of your records and/or what to do with them, it would be helpful to know yourself better. Sit down and think awhile. When the attack of T.C. subsides and your mind cools, ask: What are my motives? How far do I really want to go? What sort of 78 rpm type am I? When all is said and done, you will probably find that you fall into one of the classifications below:

Type One: Your head clears and you pull yourslf together. In a fit of revulsion you reassemble the 78's in a warped heap, feeling guilty that you even considered wasting time on such inferior merchandise. If they do not come back in style in a year or so—out they go. Maybe the garbageman will like John McCormack.

Type Two: You are pleased to have 78's but feel no burning desire to do more than leave them in a cardboard box, out of sight. You might play one or two every six months. They are conversation pieces that are not central to your overall life style. Questions of market value do not concern you. You would not miss them particularly. And they sound awful on the family stereo.

Type Three: You are moderately concerned about 78's and wish to make some sense of your collection, casually and informally. You would like to learn about their comparative worth, the artists who made them, and wish to prevent further decay by storing them properly. Playing 78's gives you a good feeling. You may add to your modest collection now and then when you come across a familiar "oldie" at a flea market—but yours is a personal, non-commercial hobby with no organized blueprint for the future of your 78's.

Type Four: You wish to amass a substantial (up to 1,000-item) collection of 78's that is representative rather than comprehensive. You fill in gaps carefully and gradually with quality discs procured from reliable dealers. Perhaps you wish to specialize in one label, one orchestra, one time-period, or one mode of popular music (jazz, swing, blues, bop, etc.) rather than collect everything within reach. You probably have a sense of history and recognize that records often reflect the times in which they were made.

Type Five: You wish to deal in records as an entrepreneur for whatever financial and mental profit may be made. You feel good at two times; when you find a valuable item, and when you trade or sell it off. Collecting for aesthetic or historical reasons is not the basic purpose. It is a means to a logical end—selling records to people who need them—and to do that successfully you must amass a very large, premier stock that will satisfy consumer demands. You are not motivated by nostalgia or any other impractical sentiments. 78's are a legitimate business enterprise and little more, although you may have your favorite records within your own collection.

If you see yourself as a Type One then this book may not be of interest at all. Type Fives are professionals who have already mastered 78's at the corporate level, but may not have the time (or the desire) to research some of the more exotic aspects of 78 rpm history. If you are a Five, this brief guide will save a great deal of valuable time and, perhaps, bring a new dimension to your stock in trade. Types Two, Three, and Four may benefit most from this material. As a Type Four, myself, I can see how my amateur colleagues could use this guide as a way to enhance their understanding of 78's, both as a physical property and a cultural phenomenon. If you still get excited when you hear old sounds on 78, still keep a sharp eye out for discs at secondhand sales, and if you and your friends like to drag out 78's and dance every once in awhile—then you will want this guide around the house.

Facing up to who you are and how far you wish to go with 78's is important, but there are some mundane aspects relating to records that must be confronted, also.

In one way, at least, old discs are just like any other collectibles: They have to be of acceptable quality to the consumer-collector. When 78's are not in top condition (and they are not, as a rule) they neither sell nor play very well. You are blessed if your records have been standing on their edges in storage albums, or sleeve jackets, in a temperate climate. Unfortunately, it is more common to find them flapjacked atop one another, without benefit of insulation, near a furnace or a leaky pipe.

How do you judge the relative condition of 78's? Since 1950 record aficionados have employed a five-part standard on which there is general agreement. You may consult the criteria in Steve Propes', *Those Oldies but Goodies: A Guide to 50's Record Collecting* (1973), but a condensed version might be helpful at this point. Starting with the most likely condition first, the yardsticks are:

Poor (P): The surface noise is so overwhelming that it renders the contents of the record meaningless; the label is obliterated; the center hole is dime-sized and frayed; cracks, chips, and deep gouges predominate. Disc is best suited to playing Frisbee.

Fair (F): The physical properties of the disc are so depleted that the surface noise and the music fight it out to a draw. There is no winner. The record is exhausted and so is the listener. Scratches and deep cuts proliferate.

Good (G): Blips, tics, and bumps may intrude on the music and cause minor waffling, but the general condition is noticeably improved over (F). When the record is over you know what was on it, and are reasonably satisfied.

Very Good (**VG**): Clean grooves and clear sounds exemplify the well-preserved, carefully-handled disc. Someone cared enough to protect it from people. Reproduction fine on most record machines.

Mint (**M**): Sometimes preceded by another category, "Excellent," (M) means shiny, sharp, impeccable, and probably never played. Such a disc is rare, coveted, and (sometimes) costly. The way 78's were meant to be—virginal.

You can easily reduce any 78 from (M) to (P) in a matter of minutes, if you are so inclined, or very hostile, but to bring a (P), (F), or (G) up to a higher classification is impossible. So it is a waste of energy to attempt it. From (M) the only way is down—and with 78's, down is forever. Even an old phonograph equipped with a "scratch remover" switch cannot rejuvenate a weatherbeaten 78. If your discs hover at the levels of (P) through (G) you might want to try to replace them through a dealer, unless you have a perverse affection for distortion. While we are on the subject let me suggest some dealers who may have what you are looking for. In late years I have had business with each one and found them to be conscientious, reasonable, and reliable:

Jack's Record Cellar, P.O. Box 14068, San Francisco, CA 94114.
Robert Nichols, Box 7757, Station C, Atlanta, GA 39309.
John Sicignano, 29 Columbia Avenue, Nutley, NJ 07110.
T. M. Thibault, P.O. Box 42, Cedar Brook, NJ 08018.
Frederick P. Williams, 813 Shawnee St., Philadelphia, PA 19118.

There are dealers in all regions of the country, although they tend to cluster near the Coasts. Most of them know the contemporary market well. They will provide lists to (and correspond with) potential customers, and work at maintaining a good reputation. There are exceptions, of course, but the typical dealer is usually candid, fair, and prompt. There is honor among discophiles still.

*   *   *   *

So far, I have recommended that you decide how you feel about 78's, suggested a means of evaluating what you own, and nominated five professionals who can help you fill out your collection. In the remaining portions of this guide, I will: (A) Offer a chronological overview of the history of 78's and related industries; (B) Report on the current 78 rpm market, highlight the most sought after labels and artists, and suggest some price ranges; (C) List those records which sold a million or more copies between 1919 and 1946; (D) Give actual dates when 550 favorite 78's were recorded; (E) Further aid in determining when your discs were made via a 1908-1946 record label time chart; (F) Acknowledge nearly 100 deceased artists who contributed mightily to the enjoyment of 78's and (G) Provide sources of additional information on the great orchestras and the time in which they prospered. My hope is that you will finish this guide with renewed appreciation for the 78 rpm record, and use the guide thereafter as a reference work. If so, then my labor of love will be rewarded sufficiently.

It occurs to me that in 1977 the phonograph will be 100 years old. Edison's invention set American music off on a new course. We have all been beneficiaries. The disc record grew out of technical refinements made by creative men such as Emile Berliner and Eldridge Johnson in the 1890's. For over 60 years the disc brought popular and classical music into our homes.

Recorded music added a dimension to our lives of which we cannot imagine being deprived. Music is both a business and an art form. Without it we would be suffering even more than we are from cultural malnutrition. As David Dachs pointed out in *Variety* (January 7, 1976), recordings ". . . have become a tremendous cultural and artistic force, crossing all national boundaries and all types of societies. . . ." He suggests that we should celebrate Edison's invention with appropriate ceremonies in 1977. And so we should. Perhaps someone will remember, in this quadraphonic era, to say a few kind words for the late, generally unlamented 78 rpm record. It, too, served us well. R.I.P. 1894-1957.

Peter A. Soderbergh
Baton Rouge, Louisiana
July 4, 1976

Record Label Key

AEO (Aeolian)
APO (Apollo)
ARA (ARA)
ASH (Asch)
AUT (Autograph)
BLB (Bluebird)
BPT (Black Patti)
BRN (Brunswick)
BSW (Black Swan)
CAM (Cameo)
CAP (Capitol)
CAR (Cardinal)
CHA (Champion)
CMD (Commodore)
COL (Columbia)
COM (Comet)
CRN (Crown)
DEC (Decca)
DEL (Deluxe)
EMR (Emerson)
GEN (Gennett)
HAR (Harmony)
HMV (His Master's Voice)
HRS (Hot Record Society)

KEY (Keynote)
MAJ (Majestic)
MAN (Manor)
MEL (Melotone)
MUS (Musicraft)
OKE (Okeh)
PAR (Paramount)
PAT (Pathe')
PER (Perfect)
PHN (Parlophone)
QRS (Quality Real Special)
REG (Regal)
RGS (Regis)
ROM (Romeo)
SAV (Savoy)
SIG (Signature)
SON (Sonora)
SWG (Swing)
VAR (Varsity)
VAY (Variety)
VEL (Velvetone)
VIC (Victor)
VOC (Vocalion)

Part One

A Mini-History of Disc Records: 1877-1957

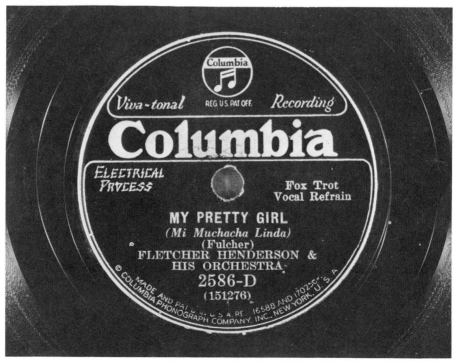

A Mini-History of Disc Records: 1877-1957

1877   December 7. John Kryesi, an employee of Thomas A. Edison's, makes the phonograph work for the first time. Edison receives patent No. 200,251 on the new machine on February 10, 1878.

1886   May 4. Patent No. 341,214 for the Gramophone is granted to Chichester Bell and Charles Tainter. The Gramophone uses wax-coated cylinders.

1887   Emile Berliner patents a machine which employs a zinc disc, rather than a cylinder, and works on perfecting the lateral stylus.

1894   American Graphophone and Columbia Phonograph companies merge under the Columbia name and the progenitor of today's Columbia Record Company is born. Berliner's U.S. Gramophone Company (1893) produces one-sided, seven-inch, two-minute discs for 50 cents apiece. Discs run at 70 rpm.

1898   Eldridge Johnson, at one time an employee of Berliner's, given patent for the "flower" horn attachment on Gramophones. Develops also a spring-driven motor for disc machines, and works on the creation of wax discs.

1901   Johnson forms his own group: Victor Talking Machine Company, and Victor Records, on March 1. Absorbs Berliner's group and incorporates Victor on October 3.

1903   April 30. Victor releases its first "Red Seal" record. Johnson signs tenor Enrico Caruso to an exclusive contract. Caruso makes *Vesti la giubba* (VIC 6001) and it goes on to sell a million copies, the first disc record to do so.

1906   August 22. Victor scoops the industry by announcing the production and sale ($200) of the Victrola, a four-foot high console with enclosed horn. Victor begins to use its "miracle asset," the trademark of the dog "Nipper" (from a painting by Francis Barraud) listening to His Master's Voice coming over a phonograph. By 1912 Victor is spending $1.2 million a year on publicity.

1908   Columbia counters with a stunning development, the two-sided disc record; thereby setting a pattern that persists for 50 years. Columbia also brings out the Grafanola to compete with the Victrola. Victor responds with two-sided popular records in 1909. Red Seal records remain one-sided until 1923.

1912   Dance mania sweeps the nation. Orchestras are formed to service the rising public demand for dance-worthy music.... Edison suspends nearly all production of cylinders and begins to manufacture thick discs....Record industry given great boost by the craze for ballroom dancing.... The "golden age" of discs begins.

1916   The bands of Jim Europe, Ted Lewis, Wilbur Sweatman, Art Hickman, King Oliver, W. C. Handy, Fate Marable, Paul Specht, Noble Sissle, Will Marion Cook, Meyer Davis, Freddie Keppard, and Coon-Sanders are touring new dance emporiums.... By the end of the year, 46 record companies are in operation.

1917   February 24. The five-piece Original Dixieland Jazz Band makes its first side for Victor in New York. *Dixie Jazz Band One-Step* (VIC 18255) sells 1.5 million copies and initiates an era of commercial jazz recordings.... Victor's assets in 1917 reach $33.2 million.

1918   World War I ends.... Paul Whiteman, Jan Garber, Vincent Lopez, George Olsen, and Leo Reisman form their orchestras.... Record industry prepares for postwar boom.

1919   Ben Selvin's orchestra records *Dardanella* for Victor and it becomes the first pop music record to sell a million copies.... Gennett Record Company of Indiana is founded.

1920   August 8. Paul Whiteman makes record (VIC 18690) of *Whispering*, which sells two million copies and moves Whiteman to the forefront of pop music for the rest of the Roaring Twenties.... Okeh and Pathe´ record companies begin operations.... November: KDKA (Pittsburgh) is first radio station to be licensed for commercial broadcasting. Record industry fails to see the significance of this at the time.

1921   Harry Pace founds first all-Negro record companies: Black Swan (New York) and Sunshine (Los Angeles).... "The Old Maestro," Ben Bernie, assembles an orchestra.

1922   By the end of the year there are 200 radio stations and three million radios in American homes.... More than 100 million records are produced and Americans spend more money on recorded music than on any other mode of entertainment.... Banner, Brunswick, Cameo, Paramount, and Perfect record companies are founded.... The New Orleans Rhythm Kings record for Gennett (GEN 4966) in September.... Paul Whiteman's *Three O'Clock in the Morning* is cut and goes on to sell two million copies by 1925.

1923   Orchestras of Guy Lombardo, Ted Weems, Ted Fio Rito, Duke Ellington, Abe Lyman, Fletcher Henderson, Bennie Moten, Erskine Tate are on the road.... Louis Armstrong's first appearance on record is with King Oliver's Jazz Band in March (PAR 12088).... Oriole Label commences.... Severe recession strikes the record business. Columbia goes into receivership in October.

1924   Victor goes into a slump.... Bell Laboratories, AT&T, and Western Electric develop a new electrical recording system which will revolutionize the disc industry.... Vernon Dalhart makes *Wreck of the Old 97* (VIC 19427), which becomes the biggest seller (over six million copies) of the acoustical recording era.... Will Osborne, Art Kassel, and Red Nichols start their bands.... Paul Whiteman's concert at Aeolian Hall (Feb. 12) ushers in the "pop jazz" movement.... There are now 694 radio stations in operation.

1925   Victor, and a revived Columbia, buy into the Western Electric system. Victor's first electrical recording (VIC 19626) goes on sale in April. The replacement of the old acoustical horn with the studio microphone enhances recording process remarkably.... The industry is rejuvenated and a new phase of disc history begins.... Orthophonic Victrolas are introduced (Nov. 2) and are a great success.... Duke Ellington cuts his first record (PER 14314) and Lawrence Welk begins his long career as a bandleader.

1926   RCA initiates the concept of the radio "network" with 19 stations.... Eldridge Johnson sells his Victor interests to several Wall Street banking firms (Dec. 7).... Victor technicians begin perfecting the automatic record changer, which is brought out in March, 1927.... Turntable speeds finally stabilize at 78 rpm.

1929   Radio sales hit $800 million. There are nearly 10 million radio sets in the U.S.... CBS Radio Network celebrates its second birthday.... Earl Hines makes his first record with his nine-man orchestra (Feb. 13), *Sweet Ella May* (VIC 22842).... Cameo company ceases production.

1932   Record industry in a deep slump due to the Depression. Sales drop to an all-time low gross of $2.5 million for the year.... Crown, Gennett, Harmony, Pathe', and Paramount labels no longer producing discs.... RCA Victor fails to follow through on the idea of a 33⅓ rpm record devised by its engineers in 1930-31.... By January, 1933 the record business is virtually defunct.

1934   A decided upturn in the record industry is noticeable.... The Decca company is formed by Jack Kapp and sells discs for 35 cents.... Jukeboxes make their presences felt across the country. Rock-Ola begins production, one year after Wurlitzer.... American Record Company buys out Columbia.... RCA Victor introduces inexpensive turntable attachment for radios, and publicizes its "high fidelity" Red Seal line as a superior product.... Bluebird Records release first discs.

1935   Benny Goodman becomes the Pied Piper of the Big Band era. "Swing" storms in on the wings of his record of *King Porter Stomp* (VIC 25090) and his sensational reception on the West Coast in August and September.... Bob Crosby, Tommy Dorsey, and Glenn Miller form their own bands and begin to record for DEC, VIC, and COL respectively.... **Downbeat** magazine starts publication.... "Your Hit Parade" debuts (Apr. 20) and a new alliance between records and radio is underway.... Annual record sales gross rises to $8.8 million.

1939   CBS, which bought up the American Record Company for $700,-000 in 1938, brings out the new Columbia label and signs Benny Goodman, Horace Heidt, Kay Kyser, and Orrin Tucker to contracts.... RCA Victor and Decca account for nearly 75% of all records sold (over 35 million total in 1939).... **Downbeat** polls place Benny Goodman, Tommy Dorsey, Glenn Miller, Bob Crosby, and Glen Gray at the top of the heap.... There are now 300,000 jukeboxes in full operation in the U.S.... The typical big band of the swing era has settled in at 14 sidemen plus the leader.... Glenn Miller is on his way to grossing $800,000 per annum, twice Goodman's income for 1937.... RCA Victor's 0-10 record player (hand-operated) is priced at $9.95, with $2.25 worth of VIC and BLB records thrown in free.

1942   The U.S.A. is at war and the record industry begins to hurt.... Bob Crosby, Dick Jurgens, Eddy Duchin, Glenn Miller are among the leaders who don uniforms.... War Production Board cuts use of shellac by 70% in Arpil.... Production of phonographs suspended.... James C. Petrillo's AFM goes on strike. Recording ban lasts until October, 1943, for DEC and CAP; to November, 1944 for VIC and COL.

1947   Expected postwar boom materializes. Over 400 million records sold (up from 275 million in 1946) and 3.4 million radio-phonographs.... Record companies formed since 1945 (King, MGM, Mercury, and Imperial) flourishing.... Rise of vocalists such as Perry Como, Frank Sinatra, and Jo Stafford beginning to undermine Big Bands' monopoly on public attention.... 78 rpm record threatened from several directions: Minnesota Mining brings out magnetic tape that can record sounds at 15,000 cycles at a speed of 7.5" per second; CBS-COL completes three years of work on a low-speed microgroove record in September.

1948   June 21. Columbia officially introduces the vinylite, 33⅓ LP disc. RCA, which had rejected Columbia's offer to share in the discovery, counters in February, 1949 with the 45 rpm record. A fascinated populace stood by while the two old foes struggled for supremacy in the marketplace. For the 78 rpm it was the Twilight of the Gods.

Epilogue (1948-1957)

By the summer of 1949 it was clear that the 33⅓ rpm disc was winning the battle. Companies who were holding back until then bought LP rights from Columbia and hastened to produce their own microgroove records. Decca moved to LP in November, 1949. Capitol manufactured both 33⅓ and 45 rpm discs that Fall. RCA Victor finally gave in in January, 1950. By the end of the year gross sales reached $172.2 million (almost double the intake for 1945).

For a year or so it appeared that the 45 rpm disc would abort, leaving RCA Victor and Capitol worse for the wear. But 45's began to develop a following at the "pop" music level in 1950-51 and other companies began to add 45's to their lines. It was Columbia's turn to capitulate. By 1954 more than 200 million 45's had been sold. RCA Victor claimed that 45's constituted over 50% of the "singles" market that year.

And what of the 78 rpm record? It was languishing, receding, and expiring. It simply could not compete with the convenience and the quality of the microgroove disc. Any doubt as to its fate was ended in 1954 when 45's passed 78's in total sales in the "pop" field. Companies were sending 45's to disc jockeys more frequently than 78's and getting positive response. Radio stations wanted discs that were durable, easily stored, and of high fidelity. Suddenly 78's seemed archaic and cumbersome.

By 1957 the 78 rpm disc had been replaced and began to fade into the recesses of public memory. The Big Bands were gone, and so was the medium that brought them into our homes for 30 years.

Part Two

78 rpm Marketplace Report

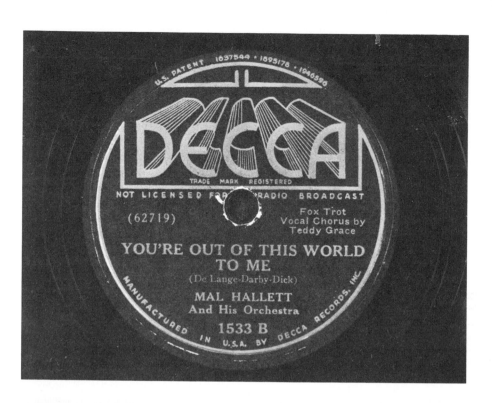

78 rpm Marketplace Report

Painful as it may be to accept, there is no necessary correlation between age and market value, with 78's, anyway. Unlike other collectibles, with 78's the acorn "the-older-the-better" simply does not apply. It is not how elderly your records are that counts but, rather, what records you have and where they fall on the (P)—(M) quality scale.

It helps to develop a modest sensitivity to when records were made as an aid in assessing their financial potential (See Part Five). If nothing else, it will alert you to whether or not they fall into the time zone in which the prize discs were released. With few exceptions the 78's that collectors and dealers pursue vigorously were made between 1915 and 1935. The records made in the twenty year period commencing with the rise of public jazz and ending prior to the mass productions of 1935-1946 appear to be the diamonds in a zircon universe. Being able to spot the right labels is a very useful skill. You may have discarded some unknowingly.

To further depress you, I have to say that if a 78 rpm record has been re-issued on 33⅓ or 45 discs, its value is, as a rule, greatly diminished (which is why no one is excited about a pile of old Carusos). Once a 78 reappears in microgroove form and becomes thereby widely available to the masses, the edge is taken off its market value. There are some exceptions, of course, the most noteworthy being the twenty-eight 78's Elvis Presley made for RCA Victor and Sun (23 and five discs, respectively) in the 1950's. And lately, 78's made by the legendary performers in the Country and Western field prior to 1953 have been commanding good prices ($5—$10).

Indeed, in the late 1970's traffic in rare 78's is very lively. As one dealer put it, "Market activity is brisk, and prices are constantly rising." To illustrate what appears to be happening at a number of levels, I have chosen to describe five typical record sellers I have known over the years. They are larger than life, but not much:

I. **Snake-oil Sam:** When you approach Sam's card table and look at his devastated records he invariably opens with: "Them are gems, your honor. And only $1 each. That's a real steal, I'll tell you. These here records are real hard to get, and they're real old, too. You can't find them kind anymore, nosirree. Just one buck...." Of course Sam hasn't the slightest notion of what he has or if they are valuable, nor does he care. He scores often enough to make it all worthwhile. As Barnum said, there's a naive customer born everyday. It could be you.

II. **Casual Carolyn:** Carolyn carries old 78's in her "antique" shop because they are there, not because she wants to. In fact, she is deeply involved with her furniture, teaspoons, and cameos—so much so that when a visitor asks about records she says, "Huh?...Oh, yes. There are some in the back, I think." To keep from having to bicker over mundanities Carolyn has a set price: 50 cents apiece regardless of artist, label, age, or condition. If you find a ruby-in-the-rough it's still a half dollar. But don't ask her any questions. She's too busy discussing antimacassars with a real customer.

III. **Gradual Gus:** Some people have a sixth sense about records. Intuitively they know that all records cannot be of equal worth, so they make an effort to sort them out by artist and condition. Gus is that type of flea. His scale is: 10 cents (P), 25—30 cents (F), 75 cents (G), $1 (VG), and $1.50 (M). He is willing to discuss records, and will negotiate on price. 78's were a part of his life, too. He understands why you are looking through his storage albums so intently. If you find something you really like, he is happy. His sources of supply are mysterious but consistent. Gus is a fellow you will visit often.

IV. **Bitter Barney.** Barney stands his ground. He is resentful and punitive. He truly does not care if anyone buys his 78's. His flat price is $2 per record no matter what. He doesn't want browsers to handle his stock. Either fork over the money or move on to the next stall. You get the distinct impression that he despises records and the aimless souls who like to see what he has for sale. Barney has no turnover. When you finally muster the courage to go back to the antique market, the very same records he had on his table six months earlier are still on display, and Barney is still scowling—almost daring you to purchase one of his 78's.

V. **Practical Phil:** You won't catch Phil mixing in the open marketplace. He is a veteran dealer who buys, sells, and trades all varieties of 78's by correspondence. You send Phil your "want list" and he will try to produce it from his stock of 15,000 old discs. His prices start at $1.50 and go up to $75. He tells you in advance where the record you want falls on the (P)—(M) spectrum. Phil knows what's going on in the 78 rpm business. And, to him, it's just a business. What you pay for is what you get. There's no need to get emotional about it. Get on Phil's mailing list and you'll learn about the relative values of jazz, pop, classical, and country 78's in short order.

When you do business with Sam, Carolyn, Gus, Barney, or Phil—or when you start looking at your own records with a keener eye—there are some labels you should make note of. Pause for a moment to reflect on what record you are about to shrug off. For example, the following labels are in vogue currently. They fall somewhere in the $5—$75 price range, according to several dealers:

Autograph	Harmony (11000 + series)
Berliner	Melotone (18000 + series)
Black Patti	Okeh (8000 series)
Black Swan	Oriole (up to 17000, and 20000 series)
Brunswick (7000 series)	Paramount
Cameo	Pathe´
Champion	Perfect (14,000 purple)

Clarion	Q.R.S.
Columbia (14000 series, black)	Rialto
Conquer	Velvetone
Electrobeam (6000 series)	Victor (23000 and 38500 series)
Gennett (5000 series)	Vocalion (blue, black, gold)

Labels aside, some 78's are in demand because of the artists who perform on them. Examples might be original discs by: Eddie Cantor; Bing Crosby (1926-1934, his pre-Decca period); Al Jolson (Columbia and Brunswick only); Helen Kane (the "Betty Boop" girl); and Sophie Tucker, the Red-Hot Mama of *Some of These Days* fame. Often, musical combinations are of interest to record dealers. You might watch for Bing Crosby singing with Paul Whiteman. (That's not so simple as it would seem. On Whiteman's *Ol' Man River*, VIC 21218, recorded 1/11/28, Crosby sings—but the label refers only to a "vocal refrain"). Alice Faye with Rudy Vallee, and Al Jolson with Guy Lombardo, are additional samples of the multiple-artist record which find favor among collectors.

Singling out the gems from the paste can be very difficult. During the 1920's, particularly, musicians frequently recorded under names other than their own. For instance, sides cut by a group called the Dixie Stompers have been pursued by collectors consistently over the years. There are very good reasons why—but the average citizen might not know what all the fuss is about. The Stompers made 16 records for the Harmony label between November, 1925 and April, 1928. In fact, "Stompers" was a pseudonym for Fletcher Henderson and his Orchestra and one cannot find much better jazz played by nine men (Coleman Hawkins, Don Redman, and Tommy Ladnier among them) than the "Stompers" produced. A number of their discs, such as *Panama* (HAR 92H, 12/22/25) and *Ain't She Sweet* (HAR 353H, 1/20/27), are minor classics. *The Wang Wang Blues* (HAR 407H, 3/23/27) was arranged by none other than Duke Ellington. Knowing these things can make a difference in the respect you have for Harmony Records the next time you are shuffling through a stack of discs. Any performance by Fletcher Henderson is worth possessing, but something by the Dixie Stompers is even better.

You notice by now that you do not see in the paragraphs above what one might describe as the typical 78, at least not the kind most Americans come across in their attics. It is almost too obvious to mention but, as a rule, the records most of us own are worth very little on today's market. Run-of-the-mill 78's released between 1935 and 1957 may be invaluable for a myriad of personal reasons, but it is unwise to project your affection for them into dollar signs too prematurely.

Indeed, the "Miracle" 78 is a very rare item which few of us have either seen or discovered in our basements. The (minor) tragedy is that we may have let some valuable discs slip through our fingers because we simply were not aware enough, or tossed them away without checking, or were led to believe that there was some real relationship between a record's popularity and its market value. Those of us who grew up in the 30's and 40's can be excused for being victims of the Victor-Columbia-Decca syndrome, I think.

As a modest step in the direction of de-programming yourself, consider carefully the section which follows. It is neither exhaustive nor comprehensive, but it is a beginning. Think of it as a way to tune up the radar, so that when valued records come within range, a bogey appears on your mental screen. Assuming that most of us notice the company name on a record before our eyes focus on the artist, I have organized this section by label. Only a small percentage of possible listings are given. The reason for presenting some of these collector's specials is to increase your sensitivity to what people who know 78's look for, not to list every selection made on every "rare" label. Perhaps after scanning this section you will want to review what discs you have in the house—or scurry over to see what Sam, Carolyn, Gus, and Barney have for sale this weekend. Good luck. Maybe one more look through that pyramid of 78's will uncover.... well, who knows?

Autograph
Merritt Brunies and His Friars Inn Orchestra
Jelly Roll Morton[1]
King Oliver

Black Patti
Frankie "Half Pint" Jaxon
Hightower's Night Hawks[2]

Black Swan
Katie Crippen
Fletcher Henderson[3]
Alberta Hunter ("Josephine Beatty")
James P. Johnson
Josie Miles
Julia Moody
Trixie Smith
Ethel Waters

Brunswick

Mildred Bailey
Bunny Berigan
Casa Loma
Bob Crosby[4]
Frank Melrose[5]
Red Nichols[6]
Red Norvo[7]
Ben Pollack
Sam Price
Louis Prima[8]
Banjo Ikey Robinson
Artie Shaw
Omer Simeon[9]
Jabbo Smith
Teddy Wilson[10]

Champion

Chicago Stompers
Turner Parrish
Wingy Manone
Frank Melrose
State Street Ramblers

Columbia

Blue Ribbon Syncopaters
Oscar "Papa" Celestin[11]
Cotton Club Orchestra[12]
Fletcher Henderson
Maggie Jones
Wingy Manone
Bessie Smith[13]
Clara Smith

Emerson

Louisiana Five

Gennett

Cook's Dreamland Orchestra[14]
Fletcher Henderson
Jelly Roll Morton
King Oliver's Creole Jazz Band[15]
Muggsy Spanier
New Orleans Rhythm Kings
Original Memphis Five[16]
Red Onion Jazz Babies[17]
Wolverines[18]

Harmony

Arkansas Travellers
Broadway Bell Hops
Dixie Stompers
Georgia Strutters
Len Herman (Red Norvo)
Ken Kenny (Red Norvo)
Mills Merry Makers
Phil Napoleon's Emperors

Melotone

Charlie Barnet
Blue Rhythm Boys
Connie's Inn Orchestra[19]
Frankie Franko and His Louisianians
Benny Goodman
Wingy Manone
Adrian Rollini and His Orchestra
Travellers[20]
Washboard Rhythm Boys

Okeh

Louis Armstrong[21]
Perry Bradford[22]
Butterbeans and Susie
Benny Carter
Chicago Footwarmers[23]
Chocolate Dandies[24]
Eddie Condon
Dorsey Brothers
Duke Ellington[25]
Troy Floyd and His Shadowland Orchestra
Goofus Five
Elizabeth Johnson
Lonnie Johnson[26]
Richard M. Jones
Bennie Moten
New Orleans Feetwarmers
Luis Russell
Hazel Smith
Hersal Thomas
Frankie Trumbauer[27]
Sippie Wallace
Clarence Williams and His Orchestra[28]
Joe Venuti

Paramount

Lovie Austin's Serenaders[29]
Jimmy Blythe
Junie Cobb's Hometown Band
Ida Cox
Charlie "Cow Cow" Davenport
Will Ezell
Fletcher Henderson
Freddie Keppard and His Jazz Cardinals
Meade Lux Lewis
Jelly Roll Morton
Jimmy O'Bryant's Washboard Wizards
King Oliver's Jazz Band[30]
Ma Rainey [31]
Trixie Smith

Perfect

Henry Allen
Cab Calloway
Chicago Loopers[32]
Buddy Christian's Jazz Rippers
Duke Ellington's Washingtonians
Fletcher Henderson
Baron Lee and His Blue Rhythm Band
Original Memphis Five
Ben Pollack[33]
The Redheads
Whoopee Makers[34]
Joe Venuti

QRS

Clarence Williams Orchestra
Earl Hines[35]

Victor

Henry Allen
Bix Beiderbecke[36]
Johnny Dodds and His Orchestra
Paul Howard's Quality Serenaders[37]
McKinney's Cotton Pickers[38]
Bubber Miley
Jelly Roll Morton's Red Hot Peppers[39]
Bennie Moten
Mound City Blue Blowers[40]
King Oliver and His Orchestra
Fats Waller
Washboard Rhythm Kings

Vocalion

Mildred Bailey
Benny Goodman's Boys
Alex Hill
The Hottentots
Dewey Jackson's Peacock Orchestra
Louisiana Rhythm Kings[41]
Jimmy McPartland
Jimmy Noone and His Orchestra(s)
Reuben Reeves and His River Boys
Luis Russell

NOTES

1. In Chicago (1924) Morton made two sides (AUT 617) accompanied by King Oliver on cornet; *Tom Cat Blues* and *King Porter Stomp*. Morton's four-piece group also cut two records (AUT 606, 607). Merritt Brunies made three discs a year later on AUT with a Chicago-based unit the same size as Morton's.

2. Trumpeter Willie Hightower's 10-piece orchestra was large for its time. On BPT 8045 (1923) he used only half his Nighthawks to record *Squeeze Me* (a very popular piano-roll number) and *Boar Hog Blues*.

3. One should always be alert for Henderson's name. Anything done by him is worth collecting, especially his 1923-1924 Club Alabam Orchestra's records on REG and, as noted earlier, HAR records by his Dixie Stompers (1925-1928). Henderson may also be found on COL, GEN, PAR, PER, and VOC labels.

4. In March, 1935 Crosby's band-to-be recorded as Clark Randall's Orchestra (BRN 7415, 7436, 7466) and as Gil Rodin's Orchestra on PER 16106, 16107. Glenn Miller played trombone on all those sides.

5. Pianist Melrose also recorded for GEN and PAR (1929-1931) as "Kansas City Frank" and "Broadway Rastus."

6. Before moving to BRN (1927-1934) Nichols' band recorded for COL, PER, and VOC as "The Redheads." He first appeared on record as Red Nichols and His Five Pennies on 12/8/26 on VOC 1069. Over the years great artists such as the Dorsey Brothers, Joe Venuti, Eddie Lang, Benny Goodman, Jack Teagarden, Gene Krupa, Glenn Miller, and Wingy Manone moved in and out of Nichols' numerous groupings.

7. Special attention should be paid to Norvo's records on which Mildred Bailey is the featured vocalist (1936-1938). Norvo and Bailey switched to the VOC label in April, 1939.

8. Prima and his New Orleans Gang (1934-1936) included names such as George Brunies, Claude Thornhill, Eddie Miller, Ray Bauduc, Pee Wee Russell, and Nappy Lamare.

9. Also known on some records as Dixie Rhythm Kings and Dixie Syncopaters (1929).

10. Wilson's band made many excellent sides between 1935 and 1939, on which were featured Benny Goodman, John Kirby, Billie Holiday, Cozy Cole, Roy Eldridge, Chu Berry, Johnny Hodges, Vido Musso, Gene Krupa, and Lester Young. Wilson's first disc for BRN (7501) was made on 7/2/35, with Billie Holiday singing *I Wished on the Moon*. His final record for BRN (8455) was cut 7/26/39.

11. Oscar "Papa" Celestin's Original Tuxedo Jazz Orchestra also cut records for OKE in 1924.

12. This Cotton Club Orchestra was actually Cab Calloway's 10-piece band, which made three records for COL in 1925. Duke Ellington did not use the "Cotton Club" designation on records until December, 1927.

13. Often accompanied by artists as important as Clarence Williams, Fletcher Henderson, Don Redman, Louis Armstrong, Coleman Hawkins, Tommy Ladnier, and James P. Johnson during the period 1923-1930.

14. C.L. "Doc" Cook's Dreamland Orchestra looms large in the exciting history of jazz dance bands of the 1920's. His orchestra, which at its height had 13 men plus Cook, was fortunate to have in it the likes of Freddie Keppard, Jimmy Noone, and Johnny St. Cyr. Recorded six sides for GEN (5360, 5373, 5374) in January, 1924; 10 more for COL (1926-1928) before disbanding in 1931.

15. Louis Armstrong, Johnny Dodds, and Baby Dodds play in Oliver's group on GEN 5132, 5133, 5134, 5135 (April, 1923).

16. Also known on many other labels as "Tennessee Ten," "Tennessee Tooters," "Cotton Pickers," and "Charleston Chasers" (1924-1929). From 1922 on, Phil Napoleon was the guiding spirit of this group.

17. Usually featuring Louis Armstrong, Lil Hardin Armstrong, Buster Bailey, Buddy Christian, and Aaron Thompson (as on GEN 5594, 5607, made in November, 1924). Sidney Bechet is with the group on GEN 5626 (December, 1924).

18. The Wolverines was the famous eight-man Chicago group in which Bix Beiderbecke played cornet (and, sometimes, piano). The band made six records for GEN (5408, 5453, 5454, 5565, 22062) at its Richmond, Indiana "studio" between March and December, 1924. George Brunies plays trombone and sings on GEN 5542. Not to be confused with Jimmy McPartland's Wolverines of 1927-1929 on BRN and VOC, an equally fine group.

19. Fletcher Henderson's orchestra in disguise on MEL 12145 and 12339 (4/25/31) and 12340 (3/11/32).

20. Otherwise known as the Dorsey Brothers Orchestra when it made six sides for MEL in 1931. Also on OKE 41260 (6/19/29). The MEL group included Glenn Miller, Bud Freeman, and Eddie Lang.

21. Armstrong's groups on OKE were variously called his "Hot Five," "Hot Seven," and "Savoy Ballroom Five" (1925-1928), and usually included his wife Lil, Kid Ory, Johnny Dodds, and Johnny St. Cyr.

22. Bradford's units recorded as: P.B. and His Jazz Phools; Mean Four Gang; on COL, HAR, PAR also (1923-1925). His VOC 15165 (11/2/25) featured Don Redman, James P. Johnson, and Louis Armstrong. Bradford's group also recorded under the "Georgia Strutters" and "Original Jazz Hounds" pseudonyms (1926-1927).

23. Either the Duke Ellington subgroup (1927), or the unit composed of Natty Dominique, Kid Ory (possibly), Johnny Dodds, Jimmy Blythe, Johnny Lindsay, and Jimmy Bertrand (1928). Ellington's side is OKE 8675; the 1928 Footwarmers cut six sides for OKE on July 2-3 (8599, 8613, 8792).

24. So many groups recorded as the "Chocolate Dandies," it is difficult to know which one you have on record. If it's OKE 8627 or 8668 you are listening to McKinney's Cotton Pickers (10/13/28); OKE 41136 is a "Dandies" unit including the Dorseys, Don Redman, and Frank Teschemacher (September, 1928); on OKE 8728 (9/18/29) some of the "Dandies" are Benny Carter, Rex Stewart, Coleman Hawkins, J.C. Higginbotham, and Fats Waller. The Blue Rhythm Band (VOC) and Buster Bailey (MEL) had "Dandies" spinoffs as well in 1931 and 1934 respectively.

25. As it is with Fletcher Henderson, anything done by Duke Ellington on BRN, CAM, COL, GEN, HAR, OKE, PER, VIC, and VOC is to be cherished. Look for his music also under the names: The Washingtonians (ROM); Lumberjacks (CAM); The Jungle Band (BRN); Six Jolly Jesters (VOC); Harlem Footwarmers (OKE); Harlem Hot Chocolates (Hit of the Week); Mills' Ten Black Berries (VEL); Harlem Music Masters (OKE); Memphis Hot Shots (HAR); Georgia Syncopators (PER); and Earl Jackson and His Musical Champions (MEL).

26. Johnson was a talented guitarist/vocalist who made over 80 records for OKE (1925-1932), and sometimes accompanied singers Victoria Spivey and Texas Alexander.

27. Between 1927 and 1929 Trumbauer's band often included a long line of great names, among them Bix Beiderbecke, Adrian Rollini, Joe Venuti, Eddie Lang, Matty Malneck, Jimmy Dorsey, Lennie Hayton, and Pee Wee Russell. His OKE releases were all in the 40000 series.

28. Also called the Blue Five and the Novelty Four, and periodically featuring Louis Armstrong, Claude Hopkins, Eddie Lang, Ed Allen, and King Oliver. Hoagy Carmichael does the vocal with Williams' Novelty Four on OKE 8645 (11/23/28).

29. Austin's group had Tommy Ladnier on trumpet (1923-1924) and Johnny Dodds in 1925-1926. Collectors will also want to be aware that Dodds played with both Jimmy Blythe and Junie Cobb in the same period.

30. Oliver made his first record in March, 1923 (PAR 12088). With him at the time were Louis Armstrong, Honore Dutray, Johnny Dodds, Baby Dodds, and Lil Hardin Armstrong. In April Oliver switched to GEN; in June to OKE; in October to COL; and back to PAR in December, 1923.

31. Ma Rainey recorded with her "Georgia Jazz Band" as well as doing solos. Accompaniment was usually provided in the latter case by Lovie Austin's Serenaders (ca. 1923-1925). Austin, Fletcher Henderson, and "Cow-Cow" Davenport sat in on piano when her Jazz Band cut sides for PAR.

32. In reality a group comprised of Bix Beiderbecke, Frankie Trumbauer, Don Murray, Carl Kress, Vic Berton, and Arthur Shutt (1927).

33. Pollack cut three discs for PER between September, 1930 and March, 1931 which are noteworthy mainly for some of the sidemen present at the sessions, e.g.: Benny Goodman, Jack Teagarden, Ray Bauduc, Sterling Bose, Eddie Miller, Babe Russin, and Nappy Lamare. One can see the nucleus of the Bob Crosby band in Pollack's 1929-1934 groups.

34. Like the "Chocolate Dandies," the Whoopee Makers is a complex issue of multiple uses of pseudonyms. Insofar as I can tell, the Whoopee Makers was a nine-man group that made about 45 sides from June, 1928 to June, 1929. Their work was distributed on 15 different labels under 21 different names (plus Whoopee Makers). The core group of WM's included: Jimmy McPartland, Jack Teagarden, Benny Goodman, Gil Rodin, Bud Freeman, Jimmy Dorsey, Ben Pollack, and several others. It should be noted that there appears to have been an Ellington subgroup by the same name operating during the same time frame on PER (15080, 15096, 15104).

35. In 1928 in Chicago, Earl Hines made four records for QRS (R7036, R7037, R7038, R7039). These piano solos are rare and priceless. On the current market a QRS can bring up to $75. Clarence Williams also is known as "Barrelhouse Five" on QRS (R7004, R7005).

36. A rare item by Beiderbecke and his orchestra is VIC 23008 (9/8/30), *I Don't Mind Walkin' in the Rain*. It is the only "orchestra" disc Bix made for VIC; Benny Goodman, Jimmy Dorsey, Pee Wee Russell, Gene Krupa, Eddie Lang, and Joe Venuti (who supposedly "directs" this particular effort) are among the band members; and any VIC records in the 23000 series are valued because so few were released. In May and September, 1930, Beiderbecke also sat in on four sides cut for VIC (38139, 23013) by Hoagy Carmichael and His Orchestra.

37. Paul Howard's was a nine-piece unit that operated out of California (1929-1930) and featured artists such as Lawrence Brown and Lionel Hampton on its five records for VIC.

38. One of the great hot bands of the pre-swing era, active from 1928 to 1933, which took its name from its business manager, William McKinney (who never played in the band). The Cotton Pickers made 53 sides for VIC. Sidemen who sat in over the years were: Don Redman (also the arranger), Benny Carter, Coleman Hawkins, Fats Waller, Rex Stewart, James P. Johnson, and Billy Taylor. Sides such as *Plain Dirt* (VIC 38097, 11/5/29) and *Zonky* (VIC 38118, 2/3/30) are selling for $5 on today's market.

39. Among Morton's Peppers during four years (1926-1930) with VIC were Kid Ory, Bubber Miley, Cozy Cole, Wilbur DeParis, Paul Barbarin, Henry Allen, and J.C. Higginbotham.

40. This exciting group's two records for VIC in 1929 (38087, 38100) starred Glenn Miller, Eddie Condon, Jack Teagarden, Coleman Hawkins, Gene Krupa, Pee Wee Russell, and Blue-Blower, Red McKenzie. Equally valuable are Blue Blowers' discs cut on the CHA label in 1935-1936 (40000 series), which feature names such as Yank Lawson, Eddie Miller, Ray Bauduc, Bunny Berigan, Carmen Mastren, Dave Tough, Dave Barbour, and, of course, McKenzie.

41. A five- or six-man group that recorded in New York (February-September, 1929). Some of the interchanging personnel were: Red Nichols, Miff Mole, Dave Tough, Glenn Miller, Tommy Dorsey, Bud Freeman, and Joe Sullivan.

Swing Classic

"HIS MASTER'S VOICE"
REG. U. S. PAT. OFF. MARCAS REGISTRADAS

VICTOR

Not Licensed for
Radio Broadcast

25570–B

SATAN TAKES A HOLIDAY—Fox Trot
(El Diablo Se Va de Fiesta)   (Larry Clinton)
Tommy Dorsey and his Orchestra
Featuring T. Dorsey, L. Jenkins, E. W. Bone, Trombones—
G. Irwin, A. Ferretti, J. Bauer, Trumpets—J. Mince, B.
Freeman, F. Stulce, M. Doty, Saxophones—C.
Mastren, Guitar—G. Traxler, Bass—
H. Smith, Piano—D. Tough, Traps

RCA Manufacturing Co., Inc.
Camden, N.J., U.S.A.

BRUNSWICK RECORD CORPORATION, NEW YORK
MADE IN U.S.A.

**FULL-RANGE
RECORDING**

Vocalion

(B 19435)   Fox Trot

A PRETTY GIRL IS LIKE A MELODY
From "Ziegfeld Follies of 1919"
—Irving Berlin—
**ART SHAW and
his NEW MUSIC**
4465

Part Three

Recording Dates for 550 Favorites, 1933-1946

THIS IS MY NIGHT TO DREAM—Fox Trot
(From Paramount film "Dr. Rhythm")
(John Burke—James Monaco)
Abe Lyman and his Orchestra
Vocal refrain by Olga Sardi
B-7366-B

B-10005-B
SUGAR FOOT STOMP—Fox Trot
(Joe Oliver-Louis Armstrong)
Jan Savitt and his Top Hatters

Recording Dates for 550 Favorites: 1933-1946

In 1970, on the assumption that people who own 78's might be interested in the ages of their records, I began to collect the data on which this section is based. I have delimited this material in a number of ways: (A) I have restricted the dates to records made during the Big Band era, suspecting that most Americans, if they have 78's at all, possess discs from that period moreso than any other. Rarer records from an earlier time are treated in Part Two; (B) For reasons of space I have listed only a fraction of the recording dates available to me, believing that readers who are curious enough to want a more exhaustive listing will be motivated to consult Charles Delauney's *New Hot Discography* and other sources (See Part Seven); and (C) I made a "judgment call" on which artists to include. Many great names do not appear here. Fans of Hal Kemp, Kay Kyser, Shep Fields, and Johnny Hodges will be disappointed, I am sure, but the line had to be drawn somewhere. I apologize in advance for omitting your favorite artist, and/or your favorite disc. My regrets, also, to the jazz purists who would not be caught dead with a big band disc in the house.

Perhaps you will be sufficiently intrigued to want to transfer some of the dates to your own record labels for posterity and safekeeping. For the serious collector, knowing something about dates can lend a historical perspective to his or her involvement with popular music. If nothing else, having actual recording dates makes for good conversation among people of like interests.

I hope the items you care most about are on the list. If not, you may wish to check the serial numbers on your records against Part Five of this text. That will start you off in the right ballpark chronologically, and rescue your 78's from total obscurity. After all, 78's have birthdays, too.

Artist/Title	Label	Date Recorded
Bert Ambrose		
Embassy Stomp	DEC 551	January 3, 1935
Hors d' Oeuvres	DEC 500	January 4, 1935
Dodging a Divorcee	DEC 457	March 20, 1935
B'wanga	DEC 726	April 15, 1935
Copenhagen	DEC 726	July 30, 1935
Night Ride	DEC 992	June 29, 1936
Wood and Ivory	DEC 972	August 12, 1936
Tarantula	DEC 1206	December 30, 1936
Cotton Pickers' Congregation	DEC 1526	July 8, 1937
Caravan	DEC 1442	July 8, 1937
Andrews Sisters		
Just a Simple Melody	DEC 1496	October 18, 1937
Bei Mir Bist Du Schoen	DEC 1562	November 24 1937
Ti-Pi-Tin	DEC 1703	February 21, 1938
Oh! Ma-Ma!	DEC 1859	June 4, 1938
Pross-Tchai	DEC 2082	September 8, 1938
Beer Barrel Polka	DEC 2462	May 3, 1939
The Jumpin' Jive	DEC 2756	September 15, 1939
Yodelin' Jive (with Bing Crosby)	DEC 2800	September 30, 1939
South American Way	DEC 2840	November 9, 1939
Louis Armstrong [1]		
You Are My Lucky Star	DEC 580	October 3, 1935
Old Man Mose	DEC 622	November 21, 1935
Music Goes 'Round and 'Round	DEC 685	January 18, 1936
I'm Putting All My Eggs in One Basket	DEC 698	February 4, 1936
Pennies from Heaven Medley (with Bing Crosby, Frances Langford, Jimmy Dorsey Orchestra)	DEC 15027 (12")	August 17, 1936
Alexander's Ragtime Band	DEC 1408	July 7, 1937
On the Sunny Side of the Street	DEC 1560	November 15, 1937
I Double Dare You	DEC 1636	January 12, 1938
When the Saints Go Marchin' In	DEC 2230	May 13, 1938
Flat Foot Floogie (with Mills Brothers)	DEC 1876	June 10, 1938
Jeepers Creepers	DEC 2267	January 18, 1939
Rockin' Chair (with Glen Gray)	DEC 2395	February 20, 1939
When It's Sleepy Time Down South (Theme)	DEC 4140	November 16, 1941

Artist/Title	Label	Date Recorded
Charlie Barnet [2]		
Knockin' at the Famous Door	BLB 10131	January 20, 1939
The Gal from Joe's	BLB 10153	February 24, 1939
Echoes of Harlem	BLB 10210	April 5, 1939
Ebony Rhapsody	BLB 10341	June 26, 1939
Cherokee (Theme)	BLB 10373	July 17, 1939
The Duke's Idea	BLB 10453	September 10, 1939
Wanderin' Blues	BLB 10721	March 21, 1940
Leapin' at the Lincoln	BLB 10774	March 21, 1940
Lament for May	BLB 10743	May 8, 1940
Pompton Turnpike	BLB 10825	July 19, 1940
Redskin Rhumba	BLB 10944	October 14, 1940
Phyllysse	BLB 11014	December 3, 1940
Good-for-Nothin' Joe (with Lena Horne)	BLB 11037	January 7, 1941
Spanish Kick	BLB 11265	June 11, 1941
Harlem Speaks	BLB 11281	August 14, 1941
Murder at Peyton Hall	BLB 11292	August 14, 1941
Drop Me Off in Harlem	DEC 18810	February 24, 1944
Skyliner	DEC 18659	August 3, 1944
New Redskin Rhumba	CAR 25001	August 12, 1946
Count Basie [3]		
Swinging at the Daisy Chain	DEC 1121	January 21, 1937
Roseland Shuffle	DEC 1141	January 21, 1937
One O'clock Jump (Theme)	DEC 1363	July 7, 1937
Topsy	DEC 1770	August 9, 1937
Sent for You Yesterday	DEC 1880	February 16, 1938
Doggin' Around	DEC 1965	June 6, 1938
Jumpin' at the Woodside	DEC 2212	August 22, 1938
Panassie Stomp	DEC 2224	November 16, 1938
Jive at Five	DEC 2922	February 4, 1939
Goin' to Chicago Blues	OKE 6244	April 10, 1941
Red Bank Boogie	COL 36766	December 6, 1944
The King	COL 37070	February 4, 1946
Bunny Berigan [4]		
Frankie and Johnnie	VIC 25616	June 25, 1937
Mahogany Hall Stomp	VIC 25622	June 25, 1937
I Can't Get Started (Theme)	VIC 36208 (12")	August 7, 1937
A Study in Brown	VIC 25653	August 18, 1937
Black Bottom	VIC 26138	December 23, 1937

Artist/Title	Label	Date Recorded

Bunny Berigan (cont.)

Russian Lullaby	VIC 26001	December 23, 1937
Can't Help Lovin' That Man	VIC 26152	December 23, 1937
High Society	VIC 26068	September 13, 1938
Jelly Roll Blues	VIC 26113	November 22, 1938
Davenport Blues	VIC 26121	November 30, 1938
There'll Be Some Changes Made	VIC 26244	March 15, 1939
Little Gate's Special	VIC 26338	March 15, 1939
Night Song	VIC 27258	November 28, 1939

Boswell Sisters

Forty Second Street	BRN 6545	April 11, 1933
The Gold-diggers' Song	BRN 6596	June 13, 1933
Don't Let Your Love Go Wrong	BRN 6929	June 21, 1934
The Object of My Affection	BRN 7348	December 10, 1934
I'm Gonna Sit Right Down and Write Myself a Letter	DEC 671	January 6, 1936
I'm Putting All My Eggs in One Basket	DEC 709	February 12, 1936

Connie Boswell

I'll Never Say 'Never Again', Again (with Bert Ambrose)	BRN 02046	July 19, 1935
On the Beach at Bali-Bali (with Bob Crosby)	DEC 829	June 9, 1936
That Old Feeling (with Ben Pollack)	DEC 1420	August 23, 1937
Martha (with Crosby's Bobcats)	DEC 1600	November 13, 1937
Deep in a Dream (with Woody Herman)	DEC 2259	January 10, 1939
Between 18th and 19th on Chestnut Street (with Bing Crosby)	DEC 2948	December 15, 1939
Yes, Indeed! (with Bing Crosby)	DEC 3689	December 13, 1940

Will Bradley

Celery Stalks at Midnight	COL 35707	January 17, 1940
Strange Cargo	COL 35545	January 17, 1940
Rhumboogie	COL 35464	March 15, 1940
Beat Me, Daddy, Eight to the Bar (Two Parts)	COL 35530	May 21, 1940
Rock-a-bye the Boogie	COL 35732	July 16, 1940
Scrub Me, Mama, with a Boogie Beat	COL 35743	September 18, 1940
Think of Me (Theme)	COL 36101	January 30, 1941
In the Hall of the Mountain King	COL 36286	May 12, 1941
All that Meat and No Potatoes	COL 36248	June 23, 1941

Artist/Title	Label	Date Recorded

Will Bradley (cont.)

Booglie Wooglie Piggy	COL 36231	June 23, 1941
Fry Me, Cookie, with a Can of Lard	COL 36719	October 16, 1941

Les Brown

Anvil Chorus	OKE 6011	January 8, 1941
Beau Night in Hotchkiss Corners	OKE 6098	February 17, 1941
Marche Slav	OKE 6199	April 8, 1941
All that Meat and No Potatoes	OKE 6323	July 1, 1941
Joltin' Joe DiMaggio	OKE 6377	August 8, 1941
Mexican Hat Dance	OKE 6696	September 17, 1941
Out of Nowhere	COL 36724	July 20, 1942
A Good Man Is Hard to Find	COL 36688	July 20, 1942

Cab Calloway [5]

Miss Otis Regrets	BRN 7504	July 2, 1935
Bugle Blues	VOC 4019	December 10, 1937
Jive	VOC 4437	August 30, 1938
Paradiddle	VOC 5467	March 8, 1940
A Ghost of a Chance	OKE 5687	June 27, 1940
Bye-bye Blues	OKE 6084	June 27, 1940
Willow, Weep for Me	OKE 6109	January 16, 1941
St. James' Infirmary	OKE 6391	July 3, 1941
Blues in the Night	OKE 6422	September 10, 1941
Virginia, Georgia and Caroline	OKE 6574	December 24, 1941
Minnie the Moocher (Theme)	OKE 6634	February 2, 1942

Benny Carter [6]

Everybody Shuffle	VOC 2870	December 13, 1934
Savoy Stampede	VOC 5112	June 29, 1939
Melancholy Lullaby (Theme)	VOC 4984	June 29, 1939
Slow Freight	VOC 5399	January 30, 1940
Night Hop	DEC 3294	May 20, 1940
Cocktails for Two	BLB 10998	November 19, 1940
Poinciana	CAP 144	October 25, 1943
Malibu	CAP 200	April 9, 1945

Casa Loma (Glen Gray) [7]

A Study in Brown	DEC 1159	February 4, 1937
Smoke Rings (Theme)	DEC 1473	July 23, 1937
Casa Loma Stomp	DEC 1412	July 23, 1937
Memories of You	DEC 1672	December 1, 1937

Artist/Title	Label	Date Recorded

Casa Loma (Glen Gray) (cont.)

Sunrise Serenade	DEC 2321	February 17, 1939
Under a Blanket of Blue	DEC 3193	September 28, 1939
No Name Jive (Two Parts)	DEC 3089	March 18, 1940
Rock Island Flag Stop	DEC 3193	April 17, 1940
It's the Talk of the Town	DEC 4292	January 15, 1942
My Heart Tells Me	DEC 18567	October 15, 1943

Bob Chester

Aunt Hagar's Blues	BLB 10513	October 12, 1939
The Octave Jump	BLB 10649	March 4, 1940
Off the Record	BLB 10865	August 1, 1940
Flinging a Whing-ding	BLB 10964	September 24, 1940
From Maine to California	BLB 11313	September 25, 1941
Harlem Confusion	BLB 11384	October 28, 1941
Sunburst (Theme)	BLB 11478	February 1, 1942
Tanning Dr. Jekyll's Hyde	BLB 11521	March 4, 1942

Larry Clinton

Midnight in the Madhouse	VIC 25697	October 15, 1937
Abba Dabba	VIC 25707	November 5, 1937
Martha	VIC 25789	February 11, 1938
My Reverie	VIC 26006	July 16, 1938
Old Folks	VIC 26056	September 1, 1938
Deep Purple	VIC 26141	December 23, 1938
In a Persian Market	VIC 26283	June 7, 1939
Study in Surrealism	VIC 26481	January 2, 1940

Nat "King" Cole [8]

Straighten Up and Fly Right	CAP 154	November 30, 1943
Sweet Lorraine	CAP 20009	December 15, 1943
It's Only a Paper Moon	CAP 20012	December 15, 1943
Sweet Georgia Brown	CAP 239	May 23, 1945
The Frim Fram Sauce	CAP 224	October 11, 1945
Route 66	CAP 256	March 15, 1946
For Sentimental Reasons	CAP 304	August 19, 1946
The Christmas Song	CAP 311	August 22, 1946
You're the Cream in My Coffee	CAP 10086	December 18, 1946

Bing Crosby

I'm an Old Cowhand	DEC 871	July 17, 1936
Too Marvelous for Words	DEC 1185	March 3, 1937

Artist/Title	Label	Date Recorded

Bing Crosby (cont.)

Smarty	DEC 1375	July 12, 1937
Bob White (with Connie Boswell)	DEC 1485	September 25, 1937
Small Fry (with Johnny Mercer)	DEC 1960	July 1, 1938
Rhythm on the River (with Connie Boswell)	DEC 3309	July 10, 1940
San Antonio Rose (with Bob Crosby)	DEC 3590	December 16, 1940
Birth of the Blues	DEC 3970	May 26, 1941
White Christmas	DEC 18429	May 25, 1942
Walkin' the Floor Over You (with Crosby's Bobcats)	DEC 18371	May 27, 1942

Bob Crosby [9]

Dixieland Shuffle	DEC 825	April 13, 1936
Come Back, Sweet Papa	DEC 896	June 12, 1936
Sugar Foot Strut	DEC 1094	June 12, 1936
Gin Mill Blues	DEC 1170	February 8, 1937
South Rampart Street Parade	DEC 15038 (12")	November 16, 1937
Yancey Special	DEC 1747	March 10, 1938
Big Crash from China	DEC 1756	March 14, 1938
Big Noise from Winnetka	DEC 2208	October 14, 1938
I'm Free	DEC 2205	October 19, 1938
Spain	DEC 3248	February 6, 1940
Sugar Foot Stomp	DEC 4390	January 27, 1942
Black Zephyr	DEC 4415	February 17, 1942

Al Donahue

Alexander's Swingin'	VOC 4562	December 2, 1938
Copenhagen	VOC 5314	December 12, 1939
Beethoven Bounce	VOC 5384	January 29, 1940
The Blue Jump	OKE 5828	September 11, 1940
Jumpin' at the Juke Box	OKE 6136	February 18, 1941

Sam Donahue

It Counts a Lot (with Count Basie)	OKE 6334	December 26, 1940
Saxaphone Sam	BLB 11169	April 11, 1941
Six Mile Stretch	BLB 11198	May 20, 1941
Flo Flo	BLB 11479	November 12, 1941
Take Five	CAP 260	April 15, 1943

Artist/Title	Label	Date Recorded

Dorsey Brothers Orchestra [10]

Artist/Title	Label	Date Recorded
Stop, Look and Listen	DEC 208	August 15, 1934
Milenberg Joys	DEC 119	August 23, 1934
Honeysuckle Rose (Two Parts)	DEC 296	August 23, 1934
Weary Blues	DEC 469	February 6, 1935
I'll Never Say 'Never Again', Again	DEC 480	May 27, 1935

Jimmy Dorsey

Artist/Title	Label	Date Recorded
Parade of the Milk Bottle Caps	DEC 941	July 7, 1936
John Silver	DEC 3334	April 29, 1938
Dusk in Upper Sandusky	DEC 1939	April 29, 1938
Swamp Fire	DEC 2918	November 27, 1939
Six Lessons from Madame LaZonga	DEC 3152	April 9, 1940
The Breeze and I	DEC 3150	April 18, 1940
Contrasts (Theme)	DEC 3198	April 30, 1940
I Understand	DEC 3585	December 9, 1940
Amapola	DEC 3629	February 3, 1941
Yours	DEC 3657	February 3, 1941
Maria Elena/Green Eyes	DEC 3698	March 19, 1941
Time Was	DEC 3859	May 19, 1941
Charleston Alley	DEC 4075	August 1, 1941
Arthur Murray Taught Me Dancing in a Hurry	DEC 4122	December 10, 1941
Tangerine	DEC 4123	December 10, 1941
Brazil	DEC 18460	July 14, 1942
At the Crossroads	DEC 18467	July 14, 1942

Tommy Dorsey [11]

Artist/Title	Label	Date Recorded
I'm Getting Sentimental Over You (Theme)	VIC 25236	October 18, 1935
Music Goes 'Round and 'Round	VIC 25201	December 9, 1935
Royal Garden Blues	VIC 25326	April 3, 1936
Song of India/Marie	VIC 25523	January 29, 1937
Smoke Gets in Your Eyes	VIC 25657	July 20, 1937
The Dipsy Doodle/Who?	VIC 25693	October 14, 1937
Little White Lies	VIC 25750	December 6, 1937
Boogie Woogie	VIC 26054	September 16, 1938
Hawaiian War Chant	VIC 26126	November 29, 1938
I'll Be Seeing You	VIC 26539	February 26, 1940
I'll Never Smile Again	VIC 26628	May 23, 1940
The One I Love	VIC 26660	June 27, 1940
Swanee River/Star Dust	VIC 27233	October 16, 1940

Artist/Title	Label	Date Recorded
Tommy Dorsey (**cont.**)		
Dolores	VIC 27317	January 20, 1941
Yes, Indeed!	VIC 27421	February 17, 1941
This Love of Mine	VIC 27508	May 28, 1941
Well, Git It!	VIC 27887	March 9, 1942
Just As Though You Were Here	VIC 27903	May 18, 1942
In the Blue of Evening	VIC 27947	June 17, 1942
There Are Such Things	VIC 27974	July 1, 1942
Opus No. 1	VIC 20-1608	November 14, 1944
Chicago	VIC 20-1728	September 7, 1945
At Sundown	VIC 20-2064	October 1, 1946
Sonny Dunham		
Memories of You	BLB 11239	July 23, 1941
Duke Ellington[12]		
In a Sentimental Mood	BRN 7461	April 30, 1935
Echoes of Harlem	BRN 7656	February 27, 1936
New Black and Tan Fantasy	BRN 8063	January 13, 1938
I Let a Song Go Out of My Heart	BRN 8108	March 3, 1938
Pyramid	BRN 8168	June 7, 1938
Mood Indigo/Solitude	COL 35427	February 14, 1940
Sophisticated Lady	COL 35556	February 14, 1940
Concerto for Cootie (Do Nothin' Till You Hear from Me)	VIC 26598	March 15, 1940
Never No Lament (Don't Get Around Much Anymore)	VIC 26610	May 4, 1940
Take the 'A' Train (Theme)	VIC 27380	February 15, 1941
I Got It Bad and That Ain't Good	VIC 27531	June 26, 1941
Perdido	VIC 27880	January 21, 1942
The 'C' Jam Blues	VIC 27856	January 21, 1942
Main Stem	VIC 20-1556	June 26, 1942
I'm Beginning to See the Light	VIC 20-1618	December 1, 1944
Black, Brown, and Beige	VIC 28-0400 (0401) (12")	December 11, 1944
Ella Fitzgerald[13]		
Out of Nowhere	DEC 2598	June 29, 1939
Baby, Won't You Please Come Home?	DEC 3186	February 15, 1940
Five O'clock Whistle	DEC 3420	September 25, 1940
Taking a Chance on Love	DEC 3490	November 8, 1940
Hello Ma! I Done It Again	DEC 3612	January 8, 1941

Artist/Title	Label	Date Recorded

Ella Fitzgerald (cont.)

Artist/Title	Label	Date Recorded
Into Each Life Some Rain Must Fall (with Ink Spots)	DEC 23356	August 30, 1944
It's Only a Paper Moon (with Delta Rhythm Boys)	DEC 23425	March 27, 1945
Stone Cold Dead in the Market (with Louis Jordan)	DEC 23546	October 9, 1945
It's a Pity to Say Goodnight (with Delta Rhythm Boys)	DEC 23670	August 29, 1946

Benny Goodman [14]

Artist/Title	Label	Date Recorded
King Porter Stomp	VIC 25090	July 1, 1935
Body and Soul (Trio)	VIC 25115	July 13, 1935
Stompin' at the Savoy	VIC 25247	January 24, 1936
I've Found a New Baby	VIC 25355	June 15, 1936
Riffin' at the Ritz	VIC 25445	October 7, 1936
Sing, Sing, Sing (Two Parts)	VIC 36205 (12")	July 6, 1937
Life Goes to a Party	VIC 25726	December 2, 1937
Don't Be That Way/One O'clock Jump	VIC 25792	February 16, 1938
And the Angels Sing	VIC 26170	February 1, 1939
Let's Dance	COL 35301	October 24, 1939
Solo Flight (with Charlie Christian)	COL 36684	March 4, 1941
Jersey Bounce	OKE 6590	January 23, 1942
Six Flats Unfurnished/Why Don't You Do Right?	COL 36652	July 27, 1942
Gotta Be This or That (Two Parts)	COL 36813	April 27, 1945

Glen Gray (See Casa Loma)

Lionel Hampton [15]

Artist/Title	Label	Date Recorded
Stompology	VIC 25601	April 14, 1937
On the Sunny Side of the Street	VIC 25592	April 26, 1937
China Stomp	VIC 25586	April 26, 1937
Ring Dem Bells	VIC 26017	January 18, 1938
Flying Home	VIC 26595	February 26, 1940
Central Avenue Breakdown/Jack the Bellboy	VIC 26652	May 10, 1940
Flying Home	DEC 18394	May 26, 1942
Hamp's Boogie Woogie	DEC 18613	March 2, 1944
Hey-Ba-Ba-Re-Bop	DEC 18754	December 1, 1945

Artist/Title	Label	Date Recorded

Coleman Hawkins [16]

Body and Soul	BLB 10523	October 11, 1939
Passin' It Around	OKE 6284	August 9, 1940

Erskine Hawkins [17]

A Study in Blue	BLB 10029	October 20, 1938
Swingin' on Lenox Avenue	BLB 10292	May 14, 1939
Gin Mill Special/Tuxedo Junction	BLB 10409	July 18, 1939
Uptown Shuffle	BLB 10504	October 2, 1939
Junction Blues	BLB 10709	June 10, 1940
After Hours	BLB 10879	June 10, 1940
Bicycle Bounce	BLB 11547	May 27, 1942
Bear Mash Blues	BLB 30-0813	June 29, 1942
Tippin' In	VIC 20-1639	January 10, 1945
Holiday For Swing	VIC 20-1794	November 21, 1945

Fletcher Henderson

Christopher Columbus	VOC 3211	March 27, 1936
Stealin' Apples	VOC 3213	March 27, 1936
Sing, Sing, Sing	VIC 25375	August 4, 1936
Jimtown Blues	VIC 25379	August 4, 1936
Stampede	VOC 3534	March 22, 1937
Sing, You Sinners	VOC 4125	October 25, 1937
Moten Stomp	VOC 4180	May 28, 1938

Woody Herman [18]

Twin City Blues	DEC 1801	April 14, 1938
Woodchopper's Ball	DEC 2440	April 12, 1939
Blues Upstairs/Blues Downstairs	DEC 2508	April 12, 1939
Farewell Blues	DEC 2582	May 24, 1939
Blues on Parade	DEC 2933	December 13, 1939
Golden Wedding	DEC 3436	November 9, 1940
Fur Trapper's Ball/Blue Flame (Theme)	DEC 3643	February 13, 1941
Bishop's Blues	DEC 3972	August 21, 1941
Blues in the Night	DEC 4030	September 10, 1941
'Tis Autumn	DEC 4095	November 13, 1941
Someone's Rocking My Dreamboat	DEC 4113	December 18, 1941
Amen	DEC 18346	April 2, 1942
Four or Five Times	DEC 18526	July 24, 1942
Milkman, Keep Those Bottles Quiet	DEC 18603	March 23, 1944
Apple Honey	COL 36803	February 1945

Artist/Title	Label	Date Recorded
Woody Herman (**cont.**)		
Bijou	COL 36861	August, 1945
Your Father's Moustache	COL 36870	September 5, 1945
Ebony Concerto(*Two Parts*)	COL 7479M (12")	August 19, 1946
Eddie Heywood		
Begin the Beguine	CMD 1514 (12")	February 19, 1944
Richard Himber		
Parade of the Bands (*Two Parts*)	VIC 25754	December 17, 1937
Earl Hines [19]		
Rosetta	DEC 337	September 12, 1934
Rhythm Sundae	VOC 3467	September 12, 1934
G. T. Stomp	BLB 10391	July 12, 1939
Grand Terrace Shuffle	BLB 10351	July 12, 1939
Father Steps In	BLB 10377	July 12, 1939
Boogie Woogie on the St. Louis Blues	BLB 10674	February 13, 1940
Deep Forest (*Theme*)	BLB 10727	February 13, 1940
Jelly Jelly	BLB 11065	December 2, 1940
Second Balcony Jump	BLB 11567	March 19, 1942
Bille Holiday		
Billie's Blues	VOC 3288	July 10, 1936
He's Funny That Way	VOC 3748	September 13, 1937
You Go to My Head	VOC 4126	May 11, 1938
I Can't Get Started	VOC 4457	September 15, 1938
Strange Fruit	CMD 526	April 20, 1939
Body and Soul	VOC 5481	February 29, 1940
St. Louis Blues	OKE 6064	October 15, 1940
Georgia on My Mind (with Eddie Heywood)	OKE 6134	March 21, 1941
Solitude	OKE 6270	May 9, 1941
Love Me or Leave Me (with Teddy Wilson)	OKE 6369	August 7, 1941
It's a Sin to Tell a Lie (with Teddy Wilson)	HAR 1075	February 10, 1942
Harry James [20]		
All or Nothing at All (with Frank Sinatra)	COL 35587	September 17, 1939

Artist/Title	Label	Date Recorded
Harry James (cont.)		
Ciribiribin (with Frank Sinatra) (Theme)	COL 35316	November 8, 1939
Concerto for Trumpet	COL 35340	November 30, 1939
Flatbush Flanagan	COL 35947	January 8, 1941
Music Makers	COL 35932	January 8, 1941
Flight of the Bumble Bee	COL 36004	February 13, 1941
Trumpet Rhapsody (Two Parts)	COL 36160	March 26/ April 28, 1941
I'll Get By	COL 36285	April 7, 1941
You Made Me Love You	COL 36296	May 20, 1941
The Mole	COL 36599	December 30, 1941
Strictly Instrumental	COL 36579	December 30, 1941
Sleepy Lagoon/Trumpet Blues	COL 36549	February 24, 1942
Easter Parade	COL 36545	February 24, 1942
Cherry	COL 36683	July 22, 1942
Prince Charming	COL 36672	July 22, 1942
I Had the Craziest Dream	COL 36659	July 22, 1942
I've Heard That Song Before	COL 36668	July 31, 1942
I'm Beginning to See the Light	COL 36758	November 21, 1944
It's Been a Long, Long Time	COL 36838	July 24, 1945
I Can't Begin to Tell You (with Betty Grable)	COL 36867	August 20, 1945
Stan Kenton [21]		
Artistry in Rhythm/Eager Beaver	CAP 159	November 19, 1943
And Her Tears Flowed Like Wine	CAP 166	May 20, 1944
Tampico	CAP 202	July, 1945
Artistry Jumps	CAP 229	October, 1945
Shoe Fly Pie and Apple Pan Dowdy	CAP 235	October, 1945
Intermission Riff	CAP 298	July, 1946
Willow Weep for Me	CAP 20087	July, 1946
John Kirby		
Sweet Georgia Brown	COL 36001	May 19, 1939
Opus 5	VOC 5048	July 28, 1939
Blues Petite	OKE 5805	May 27, 1940
Night Whispers	VIC 27667	October 7, 1941
St. Louis Blues	VIC 27926	February 11, 1942
Andy Kirk		
Moten Swing	DEC 853	March 2, 1936
Lotta Sax Appeal	DEC 1046	March 2, 1936

Artist/Title	Label	Date Recorded
Andy Kirk (cont.)		
Cloudy	DEC 1208	April 3, 1936
Mess-A-Stomp	DEC 2204	September 9, 1938
Clouds	DEC 2570	December 5, 1938
The Count/Twelfth Street Rag	DEC 18123	November 7, 1940
Gene Krupa [22]		
Wire Brush Stomp	BRN 8166	June 2, 1938
Bolero at the Savoy	BRN 8284	December 1, 1938
Apurksody (Theme)	BRN 8296	December 12, 1938
Symphony in Riffs	COL 35387	September 20, 1939
Drummin' Man	COL 35324	November 2, 1939
Boog It	COL 35415	February 12, 1940
Rhumboogie	OKE 5788	September 3, 1940
Drum Boogie	OKE 6046	January 17, 1941
Alreet	OKE 6118	March 12, 1941
Let Me Off Uptown	OKE 6210	May 8, 1941
After You've Gone	OKE 6278	June 5, 1941
Rockin' Chair	OKE 6352	July 2, 1941
Thanks for the Boogie Ride	OKE 6506	November 25, 1941
Massachusetts	OKE 6685	July 13, 1942
Leave Us Leap	COL 36802	January 22, 1945
Lover	COL 36986	October 23, 1945
Ted Lewis		
When My Baby Smiles at Me [Theme]	DEC 2054	July 16, 1938
I'm the Medicine Man for the Blues	DEC 2033	July 25, 1938
Just Around the Corner	DEC 3846	May 26, 1941
Jazz Me Blues	DEC 4272	May 26, 1941
Jimmie Lunceford [23]		
White Heat	VIC 24568	January 26, 1934
Jazznocracy	VIC 24522	January 26, 1934
Dream of You	DEC 765	October 29, 1934
Organ Grinder's Swing	DEC 908	August 31, 1936
Merry-go-round Broke Down	DEC 1318	June 15, 1937
For Dancers Only	DEC 1340	June 15, 1937
Margie	DEC 1617	January 6, 1938
Uptown Blues	VOC 5362	December 14, 1939
Battle Axe	DEC 3807	March 26, 1941
Yard Dog Mazurka	DEC 4032	August 26, 1941
Blues in the Night (Two Parts)	DEC 4125	December 22, 1941

Artist/Title	Label	Date Recorded
Clyde McCoy		
Sugar Blues	DEC 381	January 31, 1935
Jay McShann		
Hootie Blues	DEC 8559	April 30, 1941
Dexter Blues	DEC 8583	April 30, 1941
Lonely Boy Blues	DEC 4387	July 2, 1942
The Jumpin' Blues	DEC 4418	July 2, 1942
Eddie Miller		
Stomp, Mr. Henry Lee	CAP 170	February 4, 1944
Glenn Miller [24]		
Moonlight Serenade (Theme)	BLB 10214	April 4, 1939
Little Brown Jug	BLB 10286	April 10, 1939
In the Mood	BLB 10416	August 1, 1939
Johnson Rag	BLB 10498	November 5, 1939
Tuxedo Junction	BLB 10612	February 5, 1940
Pennsylvania 6-5000	BLB 10754	April 28, 1940
Anvil Chorus (Two Parts)	BLB 10982	December 13, 1940
Song of the Volga Boatmen	BLB 11029	January 17, 1941
Perfidia	BLB 11095	February 19, 1941
Chattanooga Choo Choo	BLB 11230	May 7, 1941
Adios	BLB 11219	June 25, 1941
Elmer's Tune	BLB 11274	August 11, 1941
String of Pearls	BLB 11382	November 3, 1941
Slumber Song	BLB 11386	November 24, 1941
White Cliffs of Dover	BLB 11397	November 24, 1941
Moonlight Cocktail	BLB 11401	December 8, 1941
Don't Sit Under the Apple Tree	BLB 11474	February 18, 1942
American Patrol	VIC 27873	April 2, 1942
Kalamazoo	VIC 27934	May 20, 1942
Juke Box Saturday Night	VIC 20-1509	July 15, 1942
Lucky Millinder		
Trouble in Mind	DEC 4041	June 27, 1941
Rock, Daniel	DEC 3956	June 27, 1941
Shout, Sister, Shout	DEC 18386	September 5, 1941
Apollo Jump	DEC 18529	September 5, 1941
Let Me Off Uptown	DEC 4099	November 6, 1941
Savoy	DEC 18353	February 18, 1942

Artist/Title	Label	Date Recorded
Lucky Millinder (cont.)		
Little John Special	BRN 03406	July 29, 1942
Hurry Hurry	DEC 18609	May 26, 1944
There's Good Blues Tonight	DEC 18835	February 26, 1946
Ozzie Nelson		
Tiger Rag	BRN 7523	June 23, 1935
Doing the Prom	BRN 7659	April 6, 1936
Peckin'	BLB 6974	May 3, 1937
Queen Isabella	BLB 7256	November 2, 1937
Sheik of Araby	BLB 7517	April 6, 1938
Maple Leaf Rag	BLB 7726	July 18, 1938
Stompin' at the Stadium	BLB 7814	September 7, 1938
Ruby Newman		
Make Believe Ballroom	VIC 25401	August 31, 1936
Ray Noble		
Chinatown, My Chinatown	VIC 25070	June 10, 1935
Dinah	VIC 25223	October 9, 1935
Cherokee	BRN 8247	October 8, 1938
Red Norvo		
It All Begins and Ends With You	BRN 7732	August 26, 1936
I've Got My Love to Keep Me Warm	BRN 7813	January 8, 1937
Please Be Kind	BRN 8088	February 10, 1938
You Leave Me Breathless	BRN 8135	May 2, 1938
Garden of the Moon	BRN 8202	July 26, 1938
Jersey Bounce	COL 36557	March 5, 1942
Ben Pollack		
Deep Jungle/Swing Out	COL 2879D	December 28, 1933
Song of the Islands	BRN 7764	September 15, 1936
Jimtown Blues	BRN 7764	September 16, 1936
Boogie Woogie	DEC 1517	September 11, 1937
Alice Blue Gown	DEC 1546	September 11, 1937
Teddy Powell		
Teddy's Boogie Woogie	DEC 2806	October 6, 1939
Feather Merchant's Ball/ *Teddy Bear Boogie*	DEC 3234	May 20, 1040

Artist/Title	Label	Date Recorded

Teddy Powell (cont.)

Bluebird Boogie Woogie	BLB 11082	January 29, 1941
Ode to Spring	BLB 11152	April 23, 1941
In Pinetop's Footsteps	BLB 11276	June 24, 1941
Serenade to a Maid	BLB 11373	November 4, 1941

Jan Savitt

Quaker City Jazz (Theme)	BLB 10005	October 21, 1938
When Buddha Smiles	DEC 2540	June 1, 1939
720 in the Books	DEC 2771	September 23, 1939
Sorcerer's Apprentice	VIC 27570	May 5, 1941
Sugar Foot Strut	VIC 27464	May 5, 1941
In the Hall of the Mountain King	VIC 27670	May 26, 1941
When the Sun Comes Out	VIC 27515	June 23, 1941
Afternoon of a Faun	VIC 27594	August 4, 1941

Raymond Scott

In a Subway Far from Ireland	COL 36221	November 30, 1939
Huckleberry Duck	COL 35363	December 21, 1939
Pretty Little Petticoat (Theme)	COL 35803	September 10, 1940

Artie Shaw [25]

Begin the Beguine	BLB 7746	July 24, 1938
Back Bay Shuffle	BLB 7759	July 24, 1938
Nightmare (Theme)	BLB 7875	September 27, 1938
Copenhagen	BLB 10054	November 17, 1938
Carioca	BLB 10124	January 23, 1939
Deep Purple	BLB 10178	March 12, 1939
One Night Stand	BLB 10202	March 17, 1939
Serenade to a Savage	BLB 10385	June 22, 1939
Oh! Lady Be Good	BLB 10430	August 27, 1939
All the Things You Are	BLB 10492	October 26, 1939
Frenesi	VIC 26542	March 3, 1940
Now We Know	VIC 26642	May 13, 1940
Summit Ridge Drive	VIC 26763	September 3, 1940
Temptation/Stardust	VIC 27230	Sept. 7/Oct. 7, 1940
Concerto for Clarinet (Two Parts)	VIC 36383 (12")	December 17, 1940
Dancing in the Dark	VIC 27335	January 23, 1941
Moonglow	VIC 27405	January 23, 1941
St. James' Infirmary (Two Parts)	VIC 27895	November 12, 1941
'S Wonderful	VIC 20-1638	January 9, 1945
September Song	VIC 20-1668	April 5, 1945

Artist/Title	Label	Date Recorded
Muggsy Spanier [26]		
That Dada Strain	BLB 10384	July 7, 1939
Dipper Mouth Blues	BLB 10506	November 10, 1939
At the Jazz Band Ball	BLB 10518	November 10, 1939
Riverboat Shuffle	BLB 10532	November 22, 1939
Jack Teagarden		
I Gotta Right to Sing the Blues (Theme)	BRN 8397	April 28, 1939
Aunt Hagar's Blues	COL 35206	July 19, 1939
Peg O' My Heart	COL 35727	August 25, 1939
Beale Street Blues	COL 35323	November 1, 1939
St. James' Infirmary	DEC 3844	May 26, 1941
A Hundred Years from Today	DEC 4317	May 26, 1941
Claude Thornhill		
Stack of Barley	OKE 6168	March 10, 1941
Traumerei	OKE 6124	March 10, 1941
Sleepy Serenade	OKE 6178	April 16, 1941
Snowfall (Theme)	COL 36268	May 26, 1941
Autumn Nocturne	COL 36435	October 6, 1941
I Found You in the Rain	COL 36431	October 6, 1941
Lullaby of the Rain	COL 36616	June 19, 1942
There's a Small Hotel	COL 36725	July 25, 1942
Fats Waller [27]		
I'm Gonna Sit Right Down and Write Myself a Letter	VIC 25044	May 8, 1935
Two Sleepy People	BLB 10000	October 13, 1938
Hold Tight	BLB 10116	January 19, 1939
Your Feet's Too Big	BLB 10500	November 3, 1939
Honeysuckle Rose	VIC 20-1580	May 13, 1941
The Jitterbug Waltz	BLB 11518	March 16, 1942
Ain't Misbehavin'	VIC 40-4003	January 23, 1945
Chick Webb [28]		
Stompin' at the Savoy	COL 2926D	May 15, 1934
Don't Be That Way	DEC 483	November 19, 1934
Holiday in Harlem	DEC 1521	October 27, 1937
Hallelujah	DEC 15039 (12")	December 17, 1937
A-Tisket, A-Tasket	DEC 1840	May 2, 1938
Undecided	DEC 2323	February 17, 1939

Artist/Title	Label	Date Recorded

Paul Whiteman

Ain't Misbehavin'	VIC 25086	July 9, 1935
Darktown Strutters' Ball	VIC 25192	July 10, 1935
Shall We Dance?	VIC 25552	March 26, 1937
Aunt Hagar's Blues	DEC 2145	September 9, 1938
Heart and Soul	DEC 2083	September 20, 1938
Jeepers Creepers	DEC 2222	December 8, 1938
Heat Wave	DEC 2697	April 6, 1939
Rose Room	DEC 2466	April 6, 1939
Travelin' Light (with Billie Holiday)	CAP 116	June 12, 1942

NOTES

1. Louis Armstrong made his debut on record in March, 1923, as cornet player with King Oliver's Jazz Band. As leader of his own orchestra he made 42 sides for OKE (April, 1930—December, 1932); 26 sides for VIC (December, 1932—April, 1933); and six sides for BRN (October, 1934) before moving to DEC (October, 1935), with whom he remained until April, 1942.

2. Charlie Barnet's first recording was *What Is Sweeter* (BAN 32876), made in New York on 10/9/33. Before he began his long association with BLB (January, 1939—January, 1942), with whom he cut 77 records, Barnet appeared on MEL, BLB, and VAR labels. He moved to DEC in April, 1942. In 1946 he switched to CAR and APO.

3. The Count's initial record under his own name was DEC 1141, *Honeysuckle Rose* (1/21/37). He made 28 discs for DEC up to February, 1939, and 44 for OKE/COL between November, 1939 and August, 1946. Basie began his career in 1929 as a pianist with Bennie Moten's Kansas City Orchestra. His first appearance on record with Moten was in October, 1929 on VIC 23037.

4. Bunny Berigan began his recording career as a band leader with BRN 7784 (*That Foolish Feeling*), made on 11/23/36. Prior to that time he played in, and led, small groups on VOC and PHN (January, 1933—June, 1936). Berigan cut 45 records for VIC before he gave up leading and became a sideman in other orchestras (November, 1939).

5. Cab Calloway's orchestra made its first record on 1/7/25 (COL 287D, *Down and Out Blues*). Over the years he cut sides for at least eight different major labels, including VIC, VOC (30 records), OKE)28 records), and the modern COL (six records from July, 1942—May, 1946). Among the sidemen who played in Calloway's band were Cozy Cole, Chu Berry, Dizzy Gillespie, and Jonah Jones.

6. On 9/18/29 Benny Carter played alto sax on The Chocolate Dandies' record of *That's How I Feel Today* (OKE 8728), thus launching a long and diverse recording career. He never settled down with any one record label for very long, cutting sides (1933-1946) for COL, VOC, BRN, HMV, DEC, CMD, CAP, DEL, RGS, and SWG, both at home and abroad.

7. The Casa Loma Orchestra made its first record in 1929 for OKE. Until it cut its initial side for DEC (199) in 1934, the group made records for BRN, MEL, and VIC which many observers believe set the modal pattern for the Swing Era. After 1933, the band was fronted by Glen Gray (Knoblaugh). Casa Loma disbanded in 1950.

8. Nat "King" Cole appeared on record for the first time with Eddie Cole's Solid Swingers on DEC 7210, *Honey Hush* (7/28/36). Four years later the King Cole Trio was formed. It was not until Cole signed with CAP in 1943 that he began to rise to prominence, however. The 24 records the Trio made for CAP between November, 1943 and December, 1946 are valued for their light jazz quality (with the exception of *The Christmas Song*).

9. Bob Crosby's orchestra made an astonishing number of records for DEC between 1935 and 1942: 209 (including sides cut by the "Bobcats"). The group's first side was *Flowers for Madam* (DEC 478, 6/1/35) and its last, appropriately enough, was *The Army Air Corps* (DEC 4374, 7/20/42). Few groups could play big band Dixieland jazz so well as Crosby's.

10. Jimmy and Tommy Dorsey's orchestra began recording in February, 1928, with *Mary Ann* (OKE 40995). For the next six years they came together periodically to cut sides for PER, DEC, BRN, COL, and MEL, employing artists such as Glenn Miller, Bunny Berigan, Joe Venuti, and Muggsy Spanier. On 8/14/34, the Dorseys began to record in earnest, making 46 discs for DEC until the brothers decided to go their respective ways in September, 1935. Their first side for DEC was *Heat Wave* (208), their last *You Are My Lucky Star* (559, 9/11/35).

11. His new orchestra formed, Tommy Dorsey cut his first of 203 records (through December, 1946) for VIC on 9/26/35: *Take Me Back to My Boots and Saddles* (25144). As a matter of interest, Frank Sinatra's recording career with Dorsey began with VIC 26518 (*The Sky Fell Down*, 2/1/40) and ended with VIC 27941, *Light a Candle in the Chapel* (7/2/42). Like Harry James, Dorsey added a string section to his orchestra in 1942, featuring them on record for the first time on *It Started All Over Again*.

12. Edward Kennedy Ellington commenced his impressive career on records in 1925 and was still active nearly 50 years later. From 1925 to 1946 his groups made sides for many companies, the longest periods being spent with BRN (1934-1939) and VIC (1940-1946), with interludes during which he recorded for COL, MAJ, VAR, SWG, and MUS. His first side for VIC (in the 1930's) was 38129 (4/11/30), *Double Check Stomp*.

13. Ella Fitzgerald and Her Savoy Eight made *Organ Grinder's Swing* on 11/18/36 (DEC 1062), and a great career began. She was 18 at the time. After Chick Webb's untimely death she took over his fine band and cut 25 records for DEC between June 1939 and July, 1941 as "Ella Fitzgerald and Her Famous Orchestra". Miss Fitzgerald retired in early 1976 after 40 years as an entertainer of the first order.

14. Before making his first side for VIC (*Hunkadola*, 25009, 4/4/35), Benny Goodman had appeared on the VOC, BRN, and MEL labels (1928-1935). His greatest years were ahead. For VIC he cut 106 records (to May, 1939), and then made another 117 for COL (to October, 1946). Many became classics of the Big Band Era. Goodman's initial side for modern COL was 35210, *There'll Be Some Changes Made* (8/10/39).

15 .After four years with Benny Goodman (1936-40), Lionel Hampton formed his own group (a sextette). By December, 1941 he had a dynamic, 16-piece orchestra and went on to make 17 records for DEC (through September, 1946). While he was with Goodman, Hampton collected outstanding artists and made many excellent sides for VIC, the first being 25527, *My Last Affair* (2/8/37). His initial side for DEC was *Just For You*, 18265, recorded on Christmas Eve 1941.

16. Coleman Hawkins' first record was made for PAT in New York on 9/29/33: *The Day You Came Along* (R 1685).

17. Before he joined BLB in September, 1938 Erskine Hawkins (The Twentieth Century Gabriel) made 10 records for VOC, commencing with his first side *It Was a Sad Night in Harlem* (3289, 7/20/36). He went on to record 40 discs for BLB (to June, 1942) and eight for VIC (to May, 1946).

18. Woody Herman, an Isham Jones alumnus, went through two phenomenal phases in a decade. His first band made 104 discs for DEC (November, 1936—December, 1944) and, in the two years following, his new "Herd" cut 24 spectacular records for COL. His bands were very different, and equally successful. First sides: for DEC, 1056, *Wintertime Dreams* (11/6/36); for COL, 36785, *Laura* (2/19/45).

19. Earl "Fatha" Hines recorded for GEN (1924), QRS (1928), OKE (1928), VIC (1929), BRN (1932-1934), VOC (1934, 1937-1938), DEC (1934-1935), BLB (1939-1942), SIG (1944), APO (1944), and ARA (1946). *Indiana* (10391, 7/12/39) was his first BLB record.

20. BRN 8038, *Jubilee* (12/1/37), marked Harry James' debut on record as leader of an eight-piece studio band. In February, 1939 he added five instruments and made eight records for BRN prior to its absorption by COL. Except for time spent at VAR (1940) James cut 70 records for COL (up to September, 1946), some of which featured Frank Sinatra, Dick Haymes, and Helen Forrest. Sinatra was vocalist on James' opening side for COL: *My Buddy*, 35242 (8/17/39).

21. On 9/11/41, in Hollywood, Stan Kenton went on record for the first time: DEC 4037, *The Nango*. But it was his performance on 18 discs for CAP (1943-1946) which brought his music to the public very forcefully. His sounds were almost impossible to ignore. Kenton's premiere on CAP: *Harlem Folk Dance* (145, 11/19/43).

22. Like Harry James, his colleague in the Benny Goodman band, Gene Krupa spent some time making sides for BRN (1938-1939) while the COL label was incubating. After 26 record dates for BRN, Krupa made his first side for COL (*Old Black Joe*, 7/5/39), was switched to OKE in April, 1940 where he produced some of his greatest music, and went back to COL with a newer sound in 1945. Combined number of records for COL/OKE (1939-1946): 92.

23. Jimmie Lunceford had a hard-driving, exciting band from start to finish. His career began on VIC in 1930. He spent eight years with DEC (1934-1938); (1941-1945), two with VOC/COL (1939-1941), and made six records for MAJ in 1946. *Sophisticated Lady* (129, 9/4/34) was the opening salvo in his productive tenure at DEC.

24. After a fairly frustrating three years making records for COL, DEC, and BRN (1935-1938), Miller signed with BLB and went on to become the symbol of the Big Band Era. He made 117 discs for BLB, and another 13 for VIC, before disbanding in September, 1942 to join the war effort. Between *My Reverie* (BLB 7653, 9/27/38) and *Rhapsody in Blue* (VIC 20-1529, 7/16/42) Miller sold (and made) millions.

25. In the Big Band decade (1936-1946) Artie Shaw made records for BRN, VOC, BLB, VIC, and MUS. No two of his orchestras were alike, but most of his music was superior. For BLB (1938-1939) he cut 42 records; for VIC (1940-1945), 62. Tony Pastor, Jerry Gray, Buddy Rich, Ray Coniff, Billy Butterfield and many other well-known musicians played for Shaw.

26. Francis "Muggsy" Spanier made his appearance on record in 1924 (GEN 5405) playing cornet with The Bucktown Five out of Chicago. He did not have his own permanent group until 1939, but his eight "Ragtime Band" sides for BLB rank high with jazz lovers. In 1942 Spanier cut four records on DEC with a 14-piece orchestra.

27. Thomas "Fats" Waller may rank third (behind Bob Crosby and Tommy Dorsey) in making the most "pop" records for a single company. Between 1924 and 1943 Waller made 186 discs for VIC/BLB (and another eight for HMV). In 20 years he cut records for other companies only eight times (all before 1927).

28. Chick Webb and his "Jungle Band" were introduced to the record-buying public on BRN 4450 (6/14/29). Not until 1934 did Webb find a home, at DEC, where he made 43 records (up to April, 1939). Ella Fitzgerald and John Kirby were with him when he began his climb to stardom; Louis Jordan joined him along the way. First side for DEC: *That Rhythm Man* (173, 9/10/34).

Part Four

78 Theme Songs from the 78 rpm Era

VICTOR

P 51-6   27285-B

SPEAK YOUR HEART—Fox Trot
(Di Lo Que Sientes)
(Herb Magidson—Allie Wrubel)
Hal Kemp and his Orchestra
Vocal refrain by Rosalind Marquis

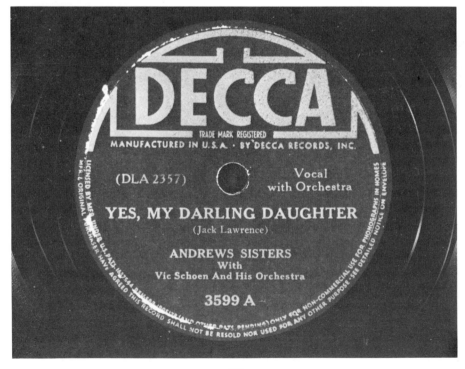

DECCA
TRADE MARK REGISTERED
MANUFACTURED IN U.S.A. · BY DECCA RECORDS, INC.

(DLA 2357)   Vocal
with Orchestra

YES, MY DARLING DAUGHTER
(Jack Lawrence)

ANDREWS SISTERS
With
Vic Schoen And His Orchestra

3599 A

78 Theme Songs From The 78 RPM Era

Nothing brings the Big Dance Bands to the forefront of the imagination so quickly as a famous theme song. A few bars of *Let's Dance, Day Dreams Come True At Night,* or *Smoke Rings* and the years fall away. Suddenly, it is November, 1939—or some other precious time we have preserved in our minds.

There we are again on the crowded floor of a college gymnasium, or pressed up against the bandstand at the Meadowbrook—oblivious to Depression, chronology, and war—drinking in every note blown our way by the travelling ambassadors of sweet and swing. Romance, tragedy, and ecstasy interweave for a moment as we go spinning back—and then the cherished images depart (as all memories do) for some uncharted region within us. It does not take much to conjure it all up again, however. Twenty seconds of Tommy Dorsey's *I'm Getting Sentimental Over You* will do the trick. It is absolutely Pavlovian.

Some theme songs—*Moonlight Serenade* being a prime example—represent much more than the aura of a particular orchestra. The young people of the 30's and 40's related so strongly to certain musical signatures that even today, should a key theme be played, they are overtaken by a tidal wave of sentiment. Identification of that magnitude says something about the impact of the Big Band ethos on the public consciousness. It was very powerful. And why not? An entire generation cut its teeth on the three R's: Records, Radio and Recreation. The Big Bands came to us that way. We played their records on the family phonograph; devoured their coast-to-coast broadcasts; and drove many miles in fragile jalopies to see them in person. The crowning point in our mounting anticipation came when the first strains of that well-known theme song burst over our sensibilities. It was an invitation to an hour or two of stroboscopic thrills. It was unforgettable.

In this section I present 78 theme songs which received a good deal of exposure between 1935 and 1945. Where possible I give record labels and dates of recording, also. In some instances I make comments which I hope will add substance to the list. You may not recognize each and every theme, but—rest assured—there is a fan for every one. Somebody out there really cares for his or her favorite, just as you do. If you have any of these discs in your collection, keep them. They may not be emeralds exactly, but they say more about the heyday of 78's than other 78 records I know. The song may be ended. These melodies linger on. As Dick Jurgens' announcer used to say: "Here's that band again!"

Artist	Theme Song
LOUIS ARMSTRONG	When It's Sleepy Time Down South[1]
MITCHELL AYRES	You Go to My Head
CHARLIE BARNET	Cherokee[2]
BLUE BARRON	Sometimes I'm Happy
COUNT BASIE	One O'Clock Jump[3]
BUNNY BERIGAN	I Can't Get Started with You[4]
BEN BERNIE	It's a Lonesome Old Town[5]
WILL BRADLEY	Think of Me[6]
LES BROWN	Leap Frog[7]
WILLIE BRYANT	It's Over Because We're Through
HENRY BUSSE	Hot Lips
BILLY BUTTERFIELD	What's New?[8]
FRANKIE CARLE	Sunrise Serenade[9]
BENNY CARTER	Melancholy Lullaby
BOB CHESTER	Sunburst
LARRY CLINTON	Dipsy Doodle[10]
BOB CROSBY	Summertime
XAVIER CUGAT	My Shawl[11]
JIMMY DORSEY	Contrasts[12]
TOMMY DORSEY	I'm Getting Sentimental over You[13]
EDDY DUCHIN	My Twilight Dream
SONNY DUNHAM	Memories of You[14]
DUKE ELLINGTON	Take the "A" Train[15]
SHEP FIELDS	Rippling Rhythm
BENNY GOODMAN	Let's Dance[16]
GLEN GRAY	Smoke Rings[17]
MAL HALLETT	Boston Tea Party
LIONEL HAMPTON	Flying Home[18]
HORACE HEIDT	I'll Love You in My Dreams

Artist	Theme Song
FLETCHER HENDERSON	Christopher Columbus[19]
WOODY HERMAN	Blue Flame[20]
RICHARD HIMBER	It Isn't Fair
EARL HINES	Deep Forest
CLAUDE HOPKINS	I Would Do Anything for You
HUDSON-DE LANGE	Eight Bars in Search of a Melody
HARRY JAMES	Ciribiribin
ISHAM JONES	You're Just a Dream Come True
JACK JENNEY	City Night
DICK JURGENS	Day Dreams Come True at Night
SAMMY KAYE	Kaye's Melody
HAL KEMP	Got a Date With an Angel
STAN KENTON	Artistry in Rhythm
HENRY KING	A Blues Serenade
WAYNE KING	The Waltz You Saved for Me
GENE KRUPA	Apurksody[21]
KAY KYSER	Thinking of You
TED LEWIS	When My Baby Smiles at Me
GUY LOMBARDO	Auld Lang Syne
JOHNNY LONG	The White Star of Sigma Nu
VINCENT LOPEZ	Nola[22]
JIMMIE LUNCEFORD	Jazznocracy[23]
FREDDY MARTIN	Bye Lo Bye Lullaby[24]
FRANKIE MASTERS	Scatterbrain
CLYDE McCOY	Sugar Blues
GLENN MILLER	Moonlight Serenade[25]
VAUGHN MONROE	Racing With the Moon
RUSS MORGAN	Does Your Heart Beat for Me?
RED NICHOLS	Wail of the Winds

Artist	Theme Song
RAY NOBLE	*The Very Thought of You*
RED NORVO	*Mr. and Mrs. Swing*
GEORGE OLSEN	*Beyond the Blue Horizon*
TONY PASTOR	*Blossoms*
BEN POLLACK	*Song of the Islands*
DON REDMAN	*Chant of the Weed*
ALVINO REY	*Blue Rey*
JAN SAVITT	*Quaker City Jazz*
RAYMOND SCOTT	*Pretty Little Petticoat*
ARTIE SHAW	*Nightmare*
BOBBY SHERWOOD	*The Elk's Parade*
FREDDIE SLACK	*Strange Cargo*
CHARLIE SPIVAK	*Star Dreams*
JACK TEAGARDEN	*I Gotta Right to Sing the Blues*[26]
CLAUDE THORNHILL	*Snowfall*
ORRIN TUCKER	*Drifting and Dreaming*
TOMMY TUCKER	*Oh, How I Love You*
CHICK WEBB	*I May Be Wrong*
LAWRENCE WELK	*Bubbles in the Wine*
PAUL WHITEMAN	*Rhapsody in Blue*

Additional discographic data on the themes listed above: Bryant (VIC 24858, 1/4/35); Chester (BLB 11478, 2/1/42); Crosby (DEC 2205, 10/21/38); Hines (BLB 10727, 2/13/40); Hudson-DeLange (BRN 7618, 1/15/36); James (COL 35316, 11/8/39); Jenney (VOC 5535, 12/6/39); Kenton (CAP 159, 11/19/43); W. King (VIC 22575, 1930); Lewis (DEC 2054, 7/16/38); McCoy (DEC 381, 1/31/35); Monroe (BLB 11070, 1941); Nichols (BLB 10408, 6/21/39); Olsen (VIC 22530, 9/5/30); Pastor (BLB 11376, 1941); Pollack (BRN 7764, 9/16/36); Redman (COL 2675D, 6/17/32); Savitt (BLB 10005, 10/21/38); Scott (COL 35803, 9/10/40); Shaw (BLB 7875, 9/27/38); Sherwood (CAP 103, 1942); Thornhill (COL 36268, 5/26/41); O. Tucker (COL 35332, 1939); and Webb (DEC 640, 10/12/35).

NOTES

1. First recorded on OKE 41504 (4/20/31) this ingratiating theme did not become readily available to the record-buying public until Armstrong cut it for DEC (4140) on 11/16/41. *Sleepy Time* abridged may also be heard on VIC 36084 (12/21/32) as one of Armstrong's Medley of Hits (12").

2. Prior to recording Ray Noble's *Cherokee* (BLB 10373) on 7/17/39 Barnet's orchestra employed *I Lost Another Sweetheart* as its theme song. *Cherokee*, of course, was more representative of the band's musical inclinations between 1939 and 1942. After 1940, Barnet sometimes used *Redskin Rhumba* as an alternate signature. On 8/12/46 he cut *Cherokee* and *New Redskin Rhumba* on CAR 25001.

3. *Jump* may be found on DEC 1363 (7/7/37) or on OKE 6634 (1/21/42). It is interesting to note that Benny Goodman's more popular version (VIC 25792) was not recorded until 2/16/38 and, it appears, was arranged by Basie.

4. First put on a 12" disc, VIC 36208 (8/7/37), this Berigan classic was subsequently (and, unsatisfactorily) dubbed onto a 10" record (VIC 25728), which a collector should avoid. Among Berigan's sidemen during this session were Steve Lipkins, George Wettling, Georgie Auld, and Joe Lippman.

5. The "Old Maestro's" closing theme, *Au Revoir-Pleasant Dreams*, was equally as prominent as *Lonesome Old Town*, perhaps due to Bernie's spoken vocal in which his famous "Yowsah" was featured. In 1951 DEC (25282) re-released both themes on one disc.

6. The original record of this beautiful ballad (COL 36101; 1/30/41) includes a bonus. On the reverse side is a jazz masterpiece, *Tea For Two*, by the Ray McKinley Quartet (McKinley, Doc Goldberg, Freddie Slack, and "Peanuts" Hucko), recorded on 1/21/41.

7. *Leap Frog* (COL 36857; 1945) was one of Brown's themes. The other, *Sentimental Journey*, with vocal by Doris Day, became one of the foremost symbols of the World War II era.

8. When Butterfield formed his orchestra in 1946, he adopted *What's New?* as his theme for good reason. While he was with the Bob Crosby band Butterfield played the trumpet solo part of Bob Haggart's lyrical composition *I'm Free* (DEC 2205; 10/19/38). Words were added to this instrumental and it became *What's New?* (*Pardon, if I'm boring you...*), a minor jazz classic.

9. By the time Frankie Carle finally formed his own band in February, 1944, *Sunrise Serenade* (his own composition) had already done more for others than for him. Glenn Miller's rendition (BLB 10214; 4/10/39), backed by *Moonlight Serenade*, sold a million copies and helped Miller capture much public attention. Glen Gray's version on DEC 2321 (2/17/39) was overwhelmed by Miller's record—even though it featured Carle on the piano for that particular session.

10. Stangely enough, Larry "The Old Dipsy Doodler" Clinton, never recorded his own theme song (and creation) during the Big Band era. The reason was this: Tommy Dorsey cut the *Dipsy Doodle* on VIC 25693 (10/14/37). In fact, Clinton arranged it for Dorsey before he organized his own orchestra in 1938. Since they were both on the VIC label, it was deemed unwise to release competitive recordings of the same tune—so Clinton could play his composition during public appearances and broadcasts only.

11. There is an earlier version of this bolero, but Cugat's 1945 record (COL 36842) with vocal by an emerging Frank Sinatra is by far more desirable from a collector's point of view.

12. Jimmy Dorsey's splendid theme was not recorded until 4/30/40 (DEC 3198). Its other side, *Perfida,* was cut on 5/10/40. Together they constitute the Dorsey band at its instrumental best.

13. George Simon was of the opinion that: "In retrospect—and in big band history—Tommy Dorsey's must be recognized as the greatest all-round dance band of them all." Simon might get an argument on that point, but few would disagree that T.D.'s touching theme song (VIC 25236; 10/17/35) ranks among the top three in pop music history.

14. Dunham's association with this song began with his trumpet solo on DEC 1672 (12/1/37), while with Glen Gray's Casa Loma orchestra. He formed his own band in February, 1940 and cut two more versions of *Memories:* VAR 8234 (March, 1940) and BLB 11239 (7/23/41), either of which is worth having if the 1937 version is unavailable.

15. For 14 years (1927-41) Ellington used *East St. Louis Toodle-oo* as his theme, recording it on BRN, COL, PAR, and DIVA. After 1941, *"A" Train* (VIC 27380; 2/15/41) predominated.

16. Goodman's first theme was a baleful interpretation of Gordon Jenkins' *Goodbye* (VIC 25215; 9/27/35). It was replaced by the cheerful, symbolic *Let's Dance* shortly after he signed with the new Columbia label. The original of the latter is COL 35301 (10/24/39) and includes performers such as Charlie Christian, Ziggy Elman, Toots Mondello, Nick Fatool, Fletcher Henderson, and Vernon Brown.

17. *Smoke Rings* was recorded by Casa Loma the first time on 3/18/32 (BRN 6289). The famous rendition was cut on 7/23/37 (DEC 1473) and featured Billy Rausch on trombone. Casa Loma had an earlier theme: *Was I to Blame for Falling in Love with You?* (BRN 6263; 2/18/32), sung by the great Kenny Sargent (who joined the band in 1931 and departed it in 1943).

18. Any one of three recordings of *Flying Home* (VIC 26595; 2/26/40; DEC 18394; 5/26/42; DEC 23639; 3/2/44) are satisfactory, but the 1942 disc was the most popular.

19. Henderson recorded *Columbus* for VOC (3211) on 3/27/36. One week earlier Benny Goodman cut a Henderson-arranged version (VIC 25279) which became much more popular, and some aspects of which he incorporated into Jimmy Mundy's arrangement of the 12" classic, *Sing, Sing, Sing* (VIC 36205; 7/6/37).

20. *Flame* (DEC 3643; 2/13/41) was superceded by *Woodchopper's Ball,* which had been recorded several years before (DEC 2440; 4/12/39).

21. *Apurksody* (Krupa spelled backwards + sody) was cut on 12/12/38 (BRN 8296). In the late war years Krupa switched to *Star Burst*.

22. Lopez' trademark was composed by Felix Arndt (b. 1882), a talented pianist who made six rare ragtime records for VIC commencing in 1912. Arndt died in the great influenza epidemic of 1918, the very year Lopez was forming his first band.

23. This driving, exciting instrumental (VIC 24522; 1/26/34), arranged by Will Hudson, served as Lunceford's theme until it was displaced by *Uptown Blues* (VOC 5362; 12/14/39).

24. *Bye Lo*, a rather turgid, uninspiring piece, gave way to the million-selling *Piano Concerto in B Flat* (*Tonight We Love*) in 1941 (BLB 11211), which catapulted Martin into the limelight he had sought since organizing his band in 1933.

25. Miller wrote this melody while he was with Ray Noble in the mid-1930's, but it was not until lyricist Mitchell Parrish tried his hand at the words that *Moonlight Serenade* took shape early in 1939. Miller recorded it on 4/4/39 (BLB 10214) and the rest is history. His alternate theme during the days of the ASCAP-BMI wars was *Slumber Song* (BLB 11386; 11/24/41), but it did not strike the public's fancy to any significant degree.

26. Teagarden's soulful theme, enhanced by his splendid vocal, was cut first on BRN 8397 (4/28/39) and then combined with *United We Swing* on OKE 6272 (10/6/39).

Part Five

Pop Record Label Time Chart, 1908-1946

*Drawn from estimates found in Charlie the Collector [Charles Hager], *When Was That Old Record Made?: Dating list for Popular 10-inch, 78-RPM Records: 1908 to 1958* (Cliffbrook, Texas, 1973, pp. 3-18; and Roger D. Kinkle, *The Complete Encyclopedia of Popular Music and Jazz, 1900-50* (New Rochelle, New York, 1974), volume Four, appendix B, 2023-2028. The description "Time Chart" is borrowed from Mr. Kinkle. I have rounded off the label numbers in most cases, since absolute precision in such matters is very difficult to attain.

Pop Record Label Time Chart, 1908-1946*

Label	Life Span	Label Numbers
BANNER	1922-35	1000—2000 (1922-27); 6000—6400 (1927-30); 0500—0900 (1929-30); 32000—33320 (1930-35).
BLUEBIRD	1933-45	5000—9100 (1933-42); 10000—11600 (1938-42); 30-0700—30-0740 (1938-45).
BRUNSWICK	1922-39	2000—4990 (1922-30); 7000—7200 (1928-31); 6000—6990 (1930-34); 7300—8460 (1934-39).
CAMEO	1922-29	280—1300 (1922-27); 8100—8400 (1927-28); 9000—9300 (1928-29).
CAPITOL	1942-	101—360 (1942-46).
CHAMPION	1927-36	15000—16700 (1927-34); 40000—50000 (1935-36).
COLUMBIA	1908-	A1—A4000 (1908-23); 1D—3170D (1923-36); 13000D—14700D (1923-32); 35200—37250 (1939-46).
COMMODORE	1938-46	500—620 (1938-46); 1500—1525 (1938-46).
CROWN	1931-33	3000—3500.
DECCA	1934-	100—4450 (1934-42); 7000—7990 (1934-42); 8500—8700 (1940-45); 18000—19000 (1939-46); 23000—23840 (1944-46).
DOMINO	1925-29	410—4220.
GENNETT	1919-30	4500—7300 (1919-30); 3000—3420 (1925-26).
GUILD	1945-46	100—150.
HARMONY	1925-31	1H—1400H.

Label	Life Span	Label Numbers
MAJESTIC	1945-47	7000—7150 (1945-46); 1100—1130 (1946).
MELOTONE	1930-38	M12000—M13280.
MERCURY	1945-	2000—8040 (1945-46).
MUSICRAFT	1944-46	100—366.
OKEH	1920-45	4230—4990 (1920-23); 8000—8930 (1921-32); 40000—41540 (1923-32); 2620—6740 (1934-45).
ORIOLE	1923-35	165—3070.
PARAMOUNT	1922-31	12000—13030 (1922-31); 20000—20680 (1922-31).
PATHE	1920-30	020100—020890 (1920-23); 036000—[0]37070 (1923-30).
PERFECT	1922-35	14000—16060 (1922-35); 12000—12980 (1922-34).
VARIETY	1936-37	500—670.
VARSITY	1938-41	8000—8400.
VICTOR	1908-	16000—28000 (1908-42); 20-1500—20-2140 (1942-46).
VOCALION	1921-40	14000—15850 (1921-29); 1000—6010 (1926-40).

Part Six

They Sold a Million: 1919-1946

Dance Orchestra
SPEED 78

B.D.5834

SLUMBER SONG—FOX-TROT
(Tepper—MacGregor)
GLENN MILLER AND HIS ORCHESTRA

CHAPPELL & CO LD
LONDON

OA.068419

THE GRAMOPHONE CO., LTD.

Decca

REG. U.S. PAT. OFF.
MARCA REGISTRADA
MANUFACTURED BY DECCA RECORDS, INC., NEW YORK, U.S.A.

(DLA 3009)
Album No. A-306
12 sides—**11**

Vocal
with Chorus
and Orchestra

WHITE CHRISTMAS
From Paramount Picture "Holiday Inn"
(Irving Berlin)
BING CROSBY
With Ken Darby Singers
And
John Scott Trotter and His Orchestra

18429 A

They Sold A Million: 1919-1946

Although being purchased one million times or more may not enhance a record's marketplace value, it does afford that disc a special place in the history of popular music. Perhaps you would like to know which of your records reached such an exalted position. You may be surprised to notice that some of the presumed "biggies" of the period do not appear on the list. There may be a number of reasons for that discrepancy: (1) The list may not be absolutely definitive; (2) In the folklore of 78's a given record's reputation as a "classic" often exceeds its actual sales; (3) The "gold record" tradition, and the sales-boosting hoopla that surrounded such an award, did not gather momentum until the late 1930's. A fair number of popular discs released before 1940, then, failed to reach the heights because the "gold record" concept had not sunk into the public consciousness; (4) The relationship between the Depression and record sales may not be direct, but it is worth noting that as the nation moved toward solvency, the number of yearly million sellers increased steadily. There were none between 1932 and 1935. By 1942 there were 19.

The material below is taken from Joseph Murrell's *Daily Mail Book of Golden Discs* (1966), a comprehensive (1903-65), invaluable reference work on which I have relied for many things. I have taken the liberty to correct a few minor errors in Murrell's text and, assuming that some of us look at an artist's name on a record label before any other feature, I have organized this honor roll alphabetically by performer(s) rather than (as Murrell did) by year of release. Only "popular" 78's, meaning those made by "pop" singers and/or dance bands, are included. Certain "country and western" discs appear because of the renewed interest in older C&W 78's (which may bring up to $10 each on the current market).

That this roster of 122 millionaires terminates with 1946 is a reflection of my view that the 78 rpm record began to fade badly when the Big Bands died in the wake of World War II. Dance bands and 78's were so interwoven that one could not survive without the other for very long. Neither has managed to make a comeback, nor can we expect them to.

So here you are. Twenty-eight years worth of million-sellers. The Golden 78's! How many do you still have—or have you thrown them all away?

Artist	Record	Label/Year
Roy Acuff	*Wabash Cannon Ball*	Columbia (1942)
Andrews Sisters[1]	*Bei Mir Bist Du Schoen*	Brunswick (1937)
	Rum and Coca Cola	Decca (1944)
Gene Austin[2]	*My Blue Heaven*	Victor (1927)
	Ramona	Victor (1928)
Gene Autry	*That Silver Haired Daddy of Mine*	Columbia (1939)
Don Azpiazu and His Orchestra	*The Peanut Vendor*	Victor (1931)
Elton Britt	*Star Spangled Banner Waving Somewhere*	Victor (1942)
Les Brown and His Orchestra	*Sentimental Journey*	Columbia (1945)
Cab Calloway and His Orchestra	*Jumpin' Jive*	Columbia (1939)
Carmen Cavallero and His Orchestra	*Chopin's Polonaise*	Decca (1945)
Perry Como	*Till the End of Time*	Victor (1945)
	If I Loved You	Victor (1945)
	Dig You Later [Hubba-Hubba-Hubba]	Victor (1945)
	Temptation	Victor (1945)
	Prisoner of Love	Victor (1946)
	I'm Always Chasing Rainbows	Victor (1946)
Bing Crosby (with Lani McIntire)	*Sweet Leilani*	Decca (1937)
(with Bob Crosby)	*San Antonio Rose*	Decca (1941)
	White Christmas	Decca (1942)
	Silent Night	Decca (1942)
	I'll Be Home for Christmas	Decca (1943)
	Sunday, Monday or Always	Decca (1943)

Artist	Record	Label/Year
(with Andrews Sisters)	*Pistol Packin' Mama*	Decca (1943)
(with Andrews Sisters)	*Jingle Bells*	Decca (1943)
	Swinging on a Star	Decca (1944)
	Too-Ra-Loo-Ra-Loo-Ra	Decca (1944)
(with Andrews Sisters)	*Don't Fence Me In*	Decca (1944)
	I Can't Begin to Tell You	Decca (1945)
(with the Jesters)	*McNamara's Band*	Decca (1946)
(with Andrews Sisters)	*South America, Take It Away*	Decca (1946)
(with Al Jolson)	*Alexander's Ragtime Band*	Decca (1946)
Al Dexter	*Pistol Packin' Mama*	Okeh (1943)
Jimmy Dorsey and His Orchestra	*Amapola*	Decca (1941)
	Green Eyes	Decca (1941)
	Maria Elena	Decca (1941)
	Besame Mucho	Decca (1943)
Tommy Dorsey and His Orchestra	*Marie*	Victor (1937)
	Boogie Woogie	Victor (1938)
	There Are Such Things	Victor (1942)
	Opus No. 1	Victor (1944)
Billy Eckstine	*Cottage for Sale*	National (1945)
	Prisoner of Love	National (1945)
Ella Fitzgerald (with Ink Spots)	*Into Each Life Some Rain Must Fall*	Decca (1944)
Will Glahe and His Orchestra	*Beer Barrel Polka*	Victor (1938)
Dick Haymes	*You'll Never Know*	Decca (1943)
Horace Heidt and His Orchestra	*Deep in the Heart of Texas*	Columbia (1941)
Woody Herman and His Orchestra	*Laura*	Columbia (1945)
Eddy Howard and His Orchestra	*To Each His Own*	Majestic (1946)
Ink Spots	*To Each His Own*	Decca (1946)
	The Gypsy	Decca (1946)

Artist	Record	Label/Year
Harry James and His Orchestra	*Ciribiribin*	Columbia (1939)
	Easter Parade	Columbia (1940)
	One O'clock Jump	Columbia (1941)
	You Made Me Love You	Columbia (1941)
	I Had the Craziest Dream	Columbia (1942)
	Moonlight Becomes You	Columbia (1942)
	I've Heard that Song Before	Columbia (1942)
Al Jolson	*Sonny Boy*	Brunswick (1928)
	April Showers	Decca (1945)
	Rockabye Your Baby with a Dixie Melody	Decca (1946)
	You Made Me Love You	Decca (1946)
	Sonny Boy	Decca (1946)
	Anniversary Song	Decca (1946)
Spike Jones and His Orchestra	*Der Fuehrer's Face*	Bluebird (1942)
	Cocktails for Two	Victor (1944)
	Glow-Worm	Victor (1946)
Louis Jordan	*Choo Choo Ch'Boogie*	Decca (1946)
Stan Kenton and His Orchestra	*Tampico*	Capitol (1945)
	Shoo-Fly Pie and Apple Pan Dowdy	Capitol (1946)
Kay Kyser and His Orchestra	*Three Little Fishies*	Columbia (1939)
	Praise the Lord and Pass the Ammunition	Columbia (1942)
	Strip Polka	Columbia (1942)
	Who Wouldn't Love You?	Columbia (1942)
	Jingle Jangle Jingle	Columbia (1942)
Guy Lombardo and His Orchestra[4]	*Humoresque*	Decca (1946)
	Christmas Island	Decca (1946)
Johnny Long and His Orchestra	*Shanty in Old Shanty Town*	Decca (1940)
Freddy Martin and His Orchestra	*Piano Concerto No. 1*	Bluebird (1941)
	White Christmas	Victor (1942)
Tony Martin	*To Each His Own*	Mercury (1946)

Artist	Record	Label/Year
Clyde McCoy and His Orchestra	Sugar Blues	Decca (1935)
Glenn Miller and His Orchestra[5]	Little Brown Jug	Bluebird (1939)
	Sunrise Serenade	Bluebird (1939)
	In the Mood	Bluebird (1939)
	Pennsylvania 6-5000	Bluebird (1940)
	Tuxedo Junction	Bluebird (1940)
	Chattanooga Choo Choo	Bluebird (1941)
	Kalamazoo	Victor (1942)
	American Patrol	Victor (1942)
Mills Brothers	Tiger Rag	Brunswick (1930)
	Paper Doll	Decca (1943)
	You Always Hurt the One You Love	Decca (1944)
Vaughn Monroe and His Orchestra	Racing with the Moon	Bluebird (1941)
	There, I've Said It Again	Victor (1945)
Red Nichols and His Five Pennies	Ida, Sweet as Apple Cider	Okeh (1927)
Pied Pipers	Dream	Capitol (1944)
Jimmie Rodgers[6]	Blue Yodel	Victor (1928)
	Brakeman's Blues	Victor (1928)
David Rose and His Orchestra	Holiday for Strings	Victor (1944)
Ben Selvin and His Orchestra	Dardanella	Victor (1919)
Artie Shaw and His Orchestra	Begin the Beguine	Bluebird (1938)
	Nightmare	Bluebird (1938)
	Back Bay Shuffle	Bluebird (1938)
	Traffic Jam	Bluebird (1939)
	Frenesi	Victor (1940)
	Stardust	Victor (1940)
	Dancing in the Dark	Victor (1940)
	Summit Ridge Drive	Victor (1940)
Dinah Shore	Blues in the Night	Victor (1941)

Artist	Record	Label/Year
Frank Sinatra (with Harry James[7])	All or Nothing at All	Columbia (1943)
	White Christmas	Columbia (1944)
Kate Smith	Rose O'Day	Columbia (1941)
Orrin Tucker and His Orchestra	Oh, Johnny, Oh	Columbia (1939)
Ernest Tubb	Walkin' the Floor over You	Decca (1941)
Chick Webb and His Orchestra[8]	A-Tisket, A-Tasket	Decca (1938)
Ted Weems and His Orchestra	Piccolo Pete	Victor (1929)
	Heartaches	Victor (1931)
Paul Whiteman and His Orchestra[9]	Whispering	Victor (1920)
	Three O'Clock in the Morning	Victor (1922)
Margaret Whiting	Moonlight in Vermont	Capitol (1944)
Bob Wills and His Texas Playboys	San Antonio Rose	Okeh (1940)

1. *Bei Mir Bist Du Schoen* sold about 100,000 copies in 1937-38 and gathered sufficient momentum over the years to qualify for the million-seller club. It is estimated that the Andrews Sisters' total sales is in the vicinity of 60 million discs.

2. *My Blue Heaven*, which turns up regularly at garage sales and flea markets, and is by no means a collector's item, is thought to have eventually sold five million copies (and at least another million in sheet music). Austin's record is a prime example of the adage: If it sold a million, it isn't worth a dime on the market.

3. *Sweet Leilani* was the first of at least 21 Crosby records which have sold over a million. In 1970 he was given a (second) platinum disc from Decca to commemorate his lifetime record sales of 300,650,000. Crosby is mentioned in the 1975 *Guiness Book of World Records* (pp. 238) as the "most successful recording artist" of all time. His rendition of *White Christmas* was the first record to achieve 100 million in sales (1970).

4. A fixture on the orchestra scene since 1923, Gaetario "Guy" Lombardo had only two more million-seller singles, *Easter Parade* (1947) and *Third Man Theme* (1950), but is credited with career total sales in excess of 100 million. Lombardo's most durable competitor, Lawrence Welk, himself a bandleader for 50 years, did not have a million-seller until 1961 (*Calcutta*).

5. Although Miller has been dead since 1944 his records and radio checks continue to do nicely. Thought by many to have had the finest commercial orchestra of the Big Band era, Miller was the first to be awarded a truly "gold" record from Bluebird/Victor in 1942 for *Chattanooga Choo Choo*. Miller's total sales are likely approaching 40 million discs (1939-75) and rising.

6. *Blue Yodel* was written by Rodgers (1897-1933) and became one of Victor's "all-time best Country and Western sellers" over the years. In 1961 Rodgers was chosen to be the first member of the Country Hall of Fame. Although his recording career began subsequent to 1946, Hank Williams (1923-53) deserves special mention at this point. In four short years (1949-52) Williams had no less than 11 million-selling records. His original sides for MGM are valued highly in today's marketplace.

7. It is said that, when it was first released in 1939, *All or Nothing at All* sold less than 10,000 copies. By 1943, both Sinatra and James were sufficiently popular to en courage Columbia to release it again, and it went over a million rapidly.

8. Much of this record's success was due to the spritely vocal by a 21-year-old woman from Virginia, Ella Fitzgerald, who went on after Webb's death in 1939 to achieve total sales of 30 million records.

9. This landmark disc, Whiteman's second record for Victor (*Avalon* was his first), eventually hit the two million level, due in large measure to the presence of *Japanese Sandman* on the reverse side. Both songs were million sheet music sellers as well.

Part Seven

78 rpm Pop Record Price Index

78 RPM Pop Record Price Index

Value is a relative quality, an elusive abstraction at best. You may prize a Guy Lombardo record so highly that its marketability does not matter to you. I may wish to collect only those discs that have obvious trade-off potential (which would exclude Lombardo, as a rule). Another person might not yet have developed a feel for what Lombardo records are worth either to himself or to others. The cliche´ one hears so often in second-hand circles—"One man's junk is another man's treasure"—certainly obtains when we speak of 78's.

Setting a working price for any collectible can be awkward because transactions involving money are always complex and subject to differing opinions. Think of how many factors are operating during a sale! Of course, negotiation (sometimes called "haggling") between seller and buyer can reduce the sales dynamic to a civilized level and result in mutual satisfaction—but both parties have to start the bidding somewhere, with some sort of price, before bargaining can commence.

The price guide below is merely a place to begin, and nothing more. I do not claim that it is the official, final word on the subject. But it may offer the collector-dealer-customer a "ballpark" figure by which he may measure what he has, wants, or can afford. Before you consult the listings, please be aware of the following points:

1. Prices fluctuate, from time to time and location to location.

2. My recommendations are based on what I have seen for sale over the years, and on recent estimates provided by Messrs. Nichols, Pierce, Sicignano, Thibault, and Williams, professional dealers to whom I am obliged.

3. Prices cited are given on the assumption that the records are in (VG) or (M) condition. Discs´ of lesser quality would command a lower price.

4. There are, no doubt, categories of records not included here which may be valuable. Simply because an artist is not mentioned does not mean his records are worthless, by any means.

5. The code "NMV" is shorthand for "no market value," meaning that the records are apparently not in demand on today's market. The typical NMV record might be worth up to $1, if it were in excellent shape, but little more. "UPS" means that, in my view, an upswing in public interest in an artist's work is observable and his or her records could be worth collecting as an investment in the future.

85

6. I have incorporated into the 303 items below most of the artists mentioned previously in Part Two, giving price ranges where possible. Part Two, plus this section, add up to a fairly reliable diagnosis of the common and uncommon market, I feel. Asterisks indicate recordings which command a higher-than-usual investment.

AARONSON, Irving	NMV, although his VIC records (1926-29) interest some collectors because of his jazz sidemen. Selected Aaronsons on VIC, numbered 20002 to 21888 might be priced at $1.
ALLEN, Henry*	For Allen's sides on PER (1933-35), at least $4; same range for his VOC releases (1935-37). On VIC $3—$8.
ALL-STAR ORCHESTRA	NMV but worth a second look because VIC 21212, 21463, and 21667 featured Miff Mole, Joe Venuti, Glenn Miller, Benny Goodman, and Tommy Dorsey. $1 for these 1927-28 discs.
ALL-STAR TRIO	NMV and no chance of improvement. No jazz, no swing, no soap.
AMBROSE, Bert	NMV for this British orchestra. Perhaps $1 for his best: *Hors d'oeuvres* (DEC 500) and *Night Ride* (DEC 992).
AMMONS, Albert*	You are operating in the $3—$5 area for his January, 1936 sides for DEC; his 1938-45 piano solos on VIC, CMD, MER, VOC same range.
ANDREWS SISTERS	UPS lately, due to nostalgia bonanza. $1.50—$2 for their classics: *Bei Mir Bist Du Schoen, Apple Blossom Time, Boogie Woogie Bugle Boy,* etc.
ARDEN-OHMAN ORCHESTRA	NMV. Big arrangements, nice twin-pianos, no sale for these VIC artists.
ARKANSAS TRAVELERS*	Five big names on HAR in 1927. Operate between $5—$8.

ARMSTRONG, Louis*   Satchmo's efforts on OKE (1924-32) move in a zone from $8 to $50. DEC discs after 1935 back down to $1.50—$2.50 level.

ARNHEIM, Gus   NMV. If you have *One More Time* (VIC 22700) with Bing Crosby on a 1931 vocal, spot it at $2.50.

AUSTIN, Gene   NMV. His VIC discs (1928-34) are everywhere but nowhere.

AUSTIN, Lovie*   Anything by Austin's Serenaders on PAR from the 20's: $4—$40.

AYRES, Mitchell   NMV. His BLB *Fashions in Music* are not fashionable anymore.

BAILEY, Mildred*   Her VIC, VOC, BRN, COL, DEC records (1931-42): $3—$5.

BARNET, Charlie   NMV as a rule. $2 for his MEL records (1933-36); $1.50 for the likes of *Cherokee, Redskin Rhumba, Pompton Turnpike.*

BARRON, Blue   NMV, no matter what.

BASIE, Count   Always a modest market for Bill Basie. Count him up to $2 for his efforts on VOC, DEC, COL, OKE, but settle for $1.50, if necessary.

BAUR, Franklyn   NMV. Swell voice, but his VIC records are flat.

BECHET, Sidney*   Most of what he recorded is worth having at $1.50—$5 on VIC, BLB, VOC.

BEIDERBECKE, Bix*   Bix is a legend, but he has appeared on LP often. $4 for his GEN, OKE, HAR records, at a minimum. Perhaps UPS, in time.

BENEKE, Tex   NMV. Post-WW II VIC releases not too inspiring. Fifty cents.

BENSON ORCHESTRA   NMV. Underrated, excellent VIC outfit, in the 25-cent bracket.

BERIGAN, Bunny*   Orchestras on VOC, BRN: $3.75—$6. VIC (1937-39): $1.50.

BERNIE, Ben   NMV for his post-1931 BRN, DEC. Earlier BRN, VOC discs: $1.50—$2.

BESTOR, Don   NMV. His VIC records (1925-27) seldom hit $1, however deserving.

BLUE RHYTHM BOYS*   Mill's Blue Rhythm groups on MEL, VIC, PER, COL (1931-36): $3.50.

BLYTHE, Jimmy*   His various 1920's groups on PAR, GEN, VOC: $7—$30.

BOSTIC, Earl   NMV. Great sax appeal but no real drawing power over $1.

BOSWELL SISTERS   Their BRN discs (1931-35) should get $1.50—$2.50 on the strength of Dorsey, Berigan, Venuti, Eddie Lang accompaniments.

BOSWELL, Connie   On DEC, supported by Woody Herman, Ben Pollack, Bob Crosby, $1—$1.50.

BRADFORD, Perry*   On COL, PAR, OKE, HAR (as "Georgia Strutters"), GEN: up to $15.

BRADLEY, Will   NMV. Classics on COL (*Down the Road Apiece, Celery Stalks at Midnight, Beat Me Daddy...*) perhaps $1.50 on a good day.

BRADSHAW, Tiny   NMV. Too bad, but a very tiny market.

BRANDWYNNE, Nat   NMV. A smooth society band with class but no status.

BREESE, Lou   NMV. Gone with the wind.

BROADWAY BELL HOPS*   Sam Lanin's 1927 band with Bix, Frankie Trumbauer on HAR: $3.50.

BROWN, Les   DEC, BLB, OKE, COL, it makes no real difference: $1.50 tops. NMV.

BYRANT, Willie   NMV, but his 1935-38 BLB, VIC, DEC records could go for $1.50. Good band.

BURR, Henry   NMV. A nickel a dozen on VIC.

BUSSE, Henry   NMV, but it would not be criminal to charge $1.50 for original DEC versions of *Hot Lips* and *When Day Is Done.*

BUTTERBEANS AND SUSIE*   Joe and Susie Edwards' OKE discs (1924, 1926) run $3.50—$15.

BUTTERFIELD, Erskine   NMV, but made good jazz on DEC (1938-42). At least $1.

BUTTERFIELD, Billy   NMV. CAP band after WW II just didn't have it.

BYRNE, Bobby   NMV. Lots of promise, good delivery, few fans. Less than $1.

CALLOWAY, Cab*   On BRN, BAN, VIC, PER (1930-36): $4. Later COL, OKE: $1.50.

CARLE, Frankie   NMV. Perhaps $1 for his two COL hits (1945-46).

CARMICHAEL, Hoagy   NMV for Hoagy on ARA, DEC. Early VIC (38139, 23013) with Bix (1930): $2.

CARTER, Benny*   On COL, VOC, DEC, BLB, CAP (1933-40): $2—$6.

CASA LOMA*   Operate in the $4—$7 zone for OKE, BRN, VIC records of the 1929-34 vintage. Slack off to $1.50—$2 for DEC of later period.

CAVALLARO, Carmen   NMV. *Polonaise* (1945) on DEC might draw one dollar.

CELESTIN, Papa*   On OKE, COL (1924-26) Papa's original tuxedo jazz band brings: $8.

CHESTER, Bob   NMV. A half-dollar will do.

CHICAGO FOOTWARMERS*	On the OKE label, two different groups. OKE 8599, 8762, 8613: a 1928 unit with Jimmy Blythe, Johnny Dodds; OKE 8675 (1927), an Ellington spinoff. Range: $7—$35.
CHICAGO LOOPERS*	PER record (1927) with Bix, Trumbauer, others: $6.
CHRISTIAN, Buddy*	His 1926-27 small units on OKE, PER usually settle in at $4.
CLARK, Buddy	Has quite a following. Superior vocalist (1936-49). $2 for work on COL.
CLINTON, Larry	NMV. *My Reverie* (VIC 26006), *Deep Purple* (VIC 26141) might hit $1.50 mark.
COBB, Junie*	PAR (1926) and VOC (1928) discs very scarce. Hot at $30.
COBURN, Jolly	NMV. 'Tis not the season to buy Jolly.
COLE, Nat "King"	NMV after 1946. Early light jazz on DEC and CAP, perhaps a light $1.50.
COLEMAN, Emil	NMV. Old debutantes may remember him. Very old debutantes.
COMO, Perry	NMV. *Till the End of Time, Prisoner of Love* could make $1.50 in super shape.
CONDON, Eddie*	1927-33 OKE, COL, VIC, BRN sides with great sidemen: $2—$7.
CONFREY, Zez	Everybody zez nix on this VIC (1920-25) pianist.
CONNIE'S INN ORCHESTRA*	Fletcher Henderson in disguise (1931-32). $6 on MEL, VIC, CRN, BRN.
COOK'S DREAMLAND ORCHESTRA*	Doc's 1923-27 band with Freddie Keppard on some sessions for OKE, GEN, COL, PAR: $15.
COON-SANDERS ORCHESTRA	Historically important, prolific, popular VIC outfit (1924-32)—but: $1.

COTTON CLUB ORCHESTRA*	Could be Cab Calloway on COL (1925), or Ellington on BRN, VIC (1928-29). In either case, $6.
COURTNEY, Del	NMV. The Del tolls not for thee.
COX, Ida*	Fine vocalist on PAR (1923-29). Wide range: $4—$20.
CRAWFORD, Jack	NMV. Little jack for big Jack.
CRAWFORD, Jesse	NMV. Terrific on the organ, terrible on the market.
CROSBY, Bing	Up to $3 for Bing's best on BRN, DEC prior to 1943. NMV rest.
CROSBY, Bob	NMV unless early (1935-38) DEC discs. Then around $2.50.
CUGAT, Xavier	NMV on VIC, COL for Coogie and company.
CUMMINS, Bernie	NMV on VIC; GEN and BRN (1923-27) efforts, maybe $1.25.
DAILEY, Frank	NMV. His Stop-and-Go orchestra never took off.
DALHART, Vernon	UPS. His *Wreck of the Old 97* (VIC 19427) is going at $4.
DAVENPORT, "Cow Cow"*	For his 1925-29 releases on OKE, PAR, VOC, CHA, VAR, GEN, and BRN: a swift $10.
DAWN, Dolly	NMV. The Dawn Patrol never came back from its mission.
DENNY, Jack	NMV despite some decent music on CAM, BRN, VIC in the 20's.
DEXTER, Al	Possible UPS, carried along on the new interest in all country artists. *Pistol Packin' Mama* (OKE) at $1.50. Don't underestimate public tastes.

DIXIE STOMPERS*	Fletcher Henderson pseudonym (1925-28) on HAR label: $7.
DODDS, Johnny*	On PAR, BRN, VOC, VIC during 1920's. Something in vicinity of $8.
DONAHUE, Al	NMV even with crooner Phil Brito thrown in.
DONAHUE, Sam	NMV. Right down there with Al. He deserves better.
DORNBERGER, Charles	NMV. Sorry, Charlie. Collectors want bands with good taste.
DORSEY BROTHERS*	Between 1928 and 1935 Tommy and Jimmy recorded for OKE, BAN, COL, VOC, BRN, and DEC. Some very exciting music from $5—$7.
DORSEY, Jimmy	NMV. Standard hits might make it to $1.50.
DORSEY, Tommy	NMV. Might top Jimmy by a quarter.
DUCHIN, Eddy	NMV. Ten very talented fingers at two cents each.
DUNHAM, Sonny	NMV. *Memories of You* worth $1.50 at least.
ECKSTINE, Billy	NMV, but his National records might bring $1.25. Fabulous singer.
ELLINGTON, Duke*	Never overlook an Ellington disc on PAT, GEN, VOC, BRN, OKE, COL, CAM, VIC. Earlier the better. Zone: $7—$30.
ENNIS, Skinnay	NMV. Three thin dimes for Skinnay on VIC.
EZELL, Will*	Tremendous pianist on PAR (1928-30). Rare, at $15—$25.
FIELDS, Shep	There are a number of hard-core fans who will pay up to $4 for a BLB (1936-1941) by Fields. NMV for his "New Music" band on BLB.

FIO RITO, Ted	NMV. Discs by Ted are dead.
FITZGERALD, Ella	Moderate interest in Ella's band on DEC (1938-42). Circa $1.50.
FLOYD, Troy*	Just a few Floyds on OKE (1928-29). Very scarce. Around $6.
FRANKO, Frankie*	Would you believe $20 for his Louisianians on MEL (1930)?
FRY, Charlie	NMV. Fry's "Million Dollar Pier" band fell short by $999,999.75.
GARLAND, Judy	NMV, but DEC records from 30's might be fixed at $1.50.
GARBER, Jan	NMV. Fallen idol of the airlanes. $1 maximum.
GEORGIA STRUTTERS*	Perry Bradford incognito (1926-27) on HAR. Up to $30.
GOLDKETTE, Jean	Look carefully at label numbers before you act. It is likely that his VIC discs between 19500 and 20995 feature sidemen such as Bix, the Dorseys, Eddie Lang, Trumbauer. Set these at $2. After 1927 (VIC 21000 and up) value drops below $1.
GOODMAN, Benny*	VOC, BRN, MEL, COL sides (1928-33) could be priced between $4—$7. His BLB, VIC, COL of later period, down to $2, plus.
GOODRICH, B.F.	NMV. The rubber never met the road for this VIC orchestra.
GORDAN, Gray	NMV. He tictocked his way into obscurity on BLB.
GRAY, Glen	See CASA LOMA, above.
GRIER, Jimmy	NMV. Nothing doing for 40 years.
HALLETT, Mal	NMV. Very popular 35 years ago. Not now.

HAMP, Johnny	NMV. Peppy VIC band in the 20's. Worth just under $1.
HAMPTON, Lionel	Borderline NMV. His VIC discs (1937-41) certainly rate $1.50, same for his later efforts on DEC. Steady interest in Hamp.
HAPPINESS BOYS	NMV. Happy days are not here again.
HAWKINS, Coleman	For Hawk's 1933-38 discs on PAR, HMV, Panachord, DEC, mostly cut in Europe, $2—$3. Dollar less for 1939-40 BLB releases.
HAWKINS, Erskine	NMV for his 1938-42 BLB, which might go at $1.25. Up to $2 on his rarer VOC discs (1936-38).
HAYMES, Dick	NMV. $1 for his 1944-50 hits like *It Might As Well Be Spring.*
HEIDT, Horace	NMV. No dawn for the Musical Knights.
HENDERSON, Fletcher*	One of the most active properties on the market. Here goes: On BSW ($2—$25); COL ($2.50—$12.50); GEN ($4—$7); PAR ($7—$35); and PER ($6—$12).
HERBECK, Ray	NMV. Brother, can you spare a dime?
HERMAN, Woody	Borderline NMV. Most DEC, COL discs (1936-46) might go at $1.50.
HIGH HATTERS	NMV for this Leonard Joy studio band on VIC.
HIGHTOWER'S NIGHT HAWKS*	Hard to locate Willie's BPT 8045 (ca. 1923). If you do: $30.
HILO HAWAIIAN ORCHESTRA	NMV. Aloha, oy.
HIMBER, Richard	NMV. Clever man, interesting bands. Invisible.

HINES, Earl*	Early work on QRS (especially), OKE, VIC, VOC, DEC may hit $30. Later BLB orchestra back down to reality at $1.50.
HITE, Les	NMV. Les did not quite hit the heights.
HODGES, Johnny	Borderline NMV. His work on BLB, VOC (1937-41): $1.50—$1.75.
HOLIDAY, Billie*	VOC and OKE offerings by Lady Day (1936-41) should be handled with care. As her legend grows, so may her 78's. Think in terms of $2—$4.
HORNE, Lena	NMV as a rule. From the hip: $1.25.
HOTTENTOTS*	Red Nichols, Miff Mole, Jimmy Dorsey were half of the Six Hottentots in 1927 on PER, BAN. In 1925 there were five on VOC. Range: $5—$8.
HOWARD, Eddy	NMV. *To Each His Own* might elicit $1.50.
HOWARD, Paul*	Howard's Quality Serenaders on VIC (1929), about $6.
HUDSON-DE LANGE	BRN discs (1936-38) perhaps $2.50. Negotiate on this good orchestra.
HUNTER, Alberta*	Look for her as "Josephine Beatty" on GEN (1924); also under her own name on OKE (1926) with Armstrong; also with Fletcher Henderson on BSW and PAR (1923); with Perry Bradford on OKE (1925); with Original Memphis Five on PAR (ca. 1923). Zone: $2—$12.50.
HUTTON, Ina Ray	NMV for the Melodears on BRN, VIC, VOC, OKE. A weak $1.25.
HYLTON, Jack	NMV. Sorry, old chap.
INK SPOTS	NMV. Splendid quartet at $1 for 1939-41 DEC classics.

INTERNATIONAL NOV- ELTY ORCHESTRA	NMV. Low level VIC studio band.
JAMES, Harry	NMV. Sides for BRN, VAR, COL (1937-46) seldom over $1.50.
JARRETT, Art	NMV as bandleader. Vocals with Ted Weems, and solos, in the 20's and 30's very effective. Ask $1.50 for COL 2672D, *Goodbye Blues*. Backed up on that by the Dorseys (6/7/32).
JAXON, Frankie*	"Half-Pints" discs on BPT, VOC (1926-33), and perhaps his 1937-39 DEC, might be placed at $5.
JENNEY, Jack	NMV, sad to say. His VOC band (1938-40) very appealing.
JOHNSON, Elizabeth*	*Empty Bed Blues* with King Oliver on OKE (1928) and others: $4—$15.
JOHNSON, James P.*	Especially 1921-23 OKE, VIC, BSW, COL (1921-23) plus other great works up to 1943: $3—$10.
JOHNSON, Jerry	NMV. Probably pseudonym for Dick Robertson. Doesn't help any.
JOHNSON, Johnny	NMV for J.J. and His Statler Pennsylvanians on VIC (1924-29).
JOHNSON, Lonnie*	Long career (1925-46) on OKE, DEC, BLB. $2—$7 (early discs).
JOHNSTON, Johnny	NMV for this CAP crooner of WW II era.
JOLSON, Al	NMV for DEC discs made after 1945. BRN sides in the 20's and 30's might tip the scale at $1.50.
JONES, Isham	NMV overall, but for BRN, VIC efforts (1922-35) a modest $1.50.

JONES, Maggie*	On COL (1924) with Armstrong, Henderson, others. Safe $5—$8.
JONES, Spike	Members of the Jones cult will offer $1.50 for his zany, unique records.
JOY, Jimmy	NMV. There is no Joy, even in Mudville.
JORDAN, Louis	On DEC (1938-46) with some spritely stuff, but NMV. Maybe $1.
JURGENS, Dick	Famous orchestra of the 30's on OKE, COL. NMV as a rule. Perhaps $1.50 for his big hits like *Day Dreams Come True at Night.*
KAHN, Roger Wolfe	NMV because few people know that between 1925-32 Venuti, Mole, Lang, Dorsey, Shaw and other lumenaries moved in and out of his VIC, COL, BRN bands. Really should be $1.25. Settle for 75 cents.
KANE'S HAWAIIANS	NMV. No war chant for this group from the 20's.
KASSEL, Art	NMV. Much appreciated in the 30's. Not up to $1, today.
KAVELIN, Al	NMV. Even his pianist, Carmen Cavallaro, cannot resurrect Al.
KAY, Beatrice	NMV. Soubrettes are out of style.
KAYE, Sammy	NMV. The old lamplighter has been snuffed. Light him for 50 cents.
KEMP, Hal	NMV. Might stretch to $1.50 for his BRN, COL, early VIC records.
KENDIS, Sonny	NMV. A quarter? A dime? Trade?
KENTON, Stan	Borderline NMV. His 1941-42 DEC records are fairly scarce. $2. CAP classics (1943-46) level off at $1.50. Everything after 1942 on LP.

KEPPARD, Freddie*	Rare Keppard and His Jazz Cardinals PAR disc (12399) of 1926: $35. He also plays on some COL, OKE, PAR sides made by Jimmy Blythe, Doc Cook and Erskine Tate during mid-20's.
KING, Wayne	NMV. The Waltz King has many devoted fans but nothing in great demand.
KIRBY, John	NMV. Made incredible music on VOC, COL, VIC, DEC. Barely $1, however.
KIRK, Andy	NMV. The clouds rolled by, leaving much joy but few big hits on BRN, DEC.
KORN KOBBLERS	NMV. Shucked.
KRUPA, Gene	Borderline NMV. Perhaps $1.50 for his spectacular cuts for BRN, VIC, PAR, COL, and OKE.
KYSER, Kay	NMV. School's out for the Old Professor.
LANDRY, Art	NMV on most of his 1924-27 VIC records. "Call of the North" discs on GEN (1923) rare items at $2—$3.
LANGFORD, Frances	NMV. Thanks for the Memory.
LANIN, Sam*	Pause before you dispense with Lanin's 1921-31 sessions for PAR, GEN, Edison, BAN, OKE, HAR, PER, or Odeon. The likes of Phil Napoleon, the Dorseys, Nichols, Mole, Goodman, and Teagarden appear in his band. For selected Lanin discs: $4—7.
LEWIS, Meade Lux*	PAR records made in 1929; DEC and VIC solos in 1936: $10—$20.
LEWIS, Ted	In the COL number series 2088D-2728D (1929-32), Lewis' band often included Goodman, Jimmy Dorsey, Fats Waller, George Brunies. For those, $2. NMV on his post-1934 DEC efforts.

LOMBARDO, Guy	NMV. For auld lang syne's sake, a good strong 50 cents.
LONG, Johnny	NMV. *Shanty in Old Shanty Town*, $1. That's about it.
LOPEZ, Vincent	NMV. His Edisons (1920), OKEs (1923-26) at $2—$3. Rest: NMV.
LOUISIANA FIVE*	Very early group (ca. 1919-20) on EMR, Edison, COL: $3.50—$6.
LOWN, Bert	NMV. Important band in 1929-31 period. Perhaps $1.
LUNCEFORD, Jimmy	NMV. Early VIC band (1930-34) discs are certainly worth $1.50—$2.
LYMAN, Abe	NMV, unless you have his BRN records (1923-33). Then, maybe, $2.
MADRIGUERA, Enric	NMV. Two for a dollar, amigo.
MALNECK, Matty	NMV. Try $1 for 1938-39 DEC, BRN, COL discs.
MANONE, Wingy*	For 1927-29 vintage COL: $5; CHA: $6. Remainder: $2.
MARTIN, Freddy	NMV. Maximum $1.50 for his big record.
MARVIN, Johnny	NMV for this prolific VIC vocalist. No one seems to remember.
MASTERS, Frankie	NMV. Zero potential.
McCOY, Clyde	NMV. *Sugar Blues* at $1.50 is the whole story.
McFARLAND TWINS	NMV. Two leaders not always better than one.
McINTYRE, Hal	NMV. A dollar for *I'm Making Believe*, then move on.

McKENZIE, Red*	Early records on VOC, OKE, COL (1924-33) have great sidemen: $3.
McKINNEY'S COTTON PICKERS*	Original VIC works (1928-31) currently moving at $4; same for reproductions (VIC 40-0114 up series). $2 for lesser quality arrangements.
McSHANN, Jay	NMV. Made some fine sides for DEC. No movement.
MELROSE, Frank*	Kansas City Frank on GEN, PAR, BRN, CHA between 1929-31: up to $35.
MERCER, Johnny	NMV even if you accentuate the positive.
MESSNER, Johnny	NMV. His music box ran down.
MILES, Josie*	On BSW, GEN in 1924 accompanied by Fletcher Henderson: $4—$8.
MILLER, Glenn	UPS possible. There are indications that a resurgence of interest in old Miller 78's may be brewing. Young people in England are discovering new things in Big Band arrangements and it might be contagious. Right now: $1.50—$2 for his best BLB performances. Be alert.
MILLINDER, Lucky	NMV even with Sister Rosetta. A delicate $1.
MILLS BROTHERS	NMV unless you find early BRN discs with Bing, Ellington. Then: $3.
MONROE, Vaughn	NMV. *Racing With the Moon* caliber hits: $1.25 on BLB.
MOONEY, Art	NMV. The four leaf clover didn't help.
MORGAN, Russ	NMV. Few hearts beat for his records.
MORTON, Jelly Roll*	Highly preferred artist among collectors. On GEN (1923-24): $40; PAR (1923-24): $20—$40; AUT (1924): $35; and VIC (1926-30): $4—$40, the earlier the better.

MOTEN, Bennie*   Keep a watch on his OKE (1923-25) and VIC (1926-32) records, the VIC numbers being in the 23000 to 24000 range. Pricing: $3—$15.

MOUND CITY BLUE BLOWERS*   Red McKenzie and other stars made exciting music on BRN, VOC, CHA, DEC, VIC, OKE for 10 years (1924-34). Zone: $2—$7.

MURRAY, Kel   NMV. No sale in the salon.

NAPOLEON, Phil*   Most discs on Edison, VIC, HAR, made between 1926-29 by his Emperors and other groups should be tabbed at $4.

NELSON, Ozzie   NMV. Oz no wizard. Sentimentalists: $1.25 for early BRN, VOC.

NEWMAN, Ruby   NMV. Few gems for Ruby.

NEW ORLEANS RHYTHM KINGS*   Hold on to your wallet. On GEN, OKE, VIC the N.O.R.K. brings from $15 to $100; the higher price for the 1922-23 GEN sides. Very rare, very expensive.

NICHOLS, Red*   Most of Red's work on Edison, BRN, VIC is worth collecting. Post-1933 BLB discs less effective. Early sides: $8, down to $2 for later ones.

NOBLE, Ray   NMV, but his 1935-37 VIC efforts are semi-classics. $1.50—$2.

NORVO, Red*   Norvo on CHA, BRN, VOC, COL from 1933 to 1942 moves in the $2.50—$8 range. Mildred Bailey on COL sides (1938-42).

O'BRYANT, Jimmy*   His Washboard Wizards on PAR (1925-26): $6—$10.

OLIVER, Joe "King"*   Prepare to spend money if you want original Olivers. King on GEN (1923): $100—$150; on PAR (1923): $75—$100; on VIC (1929-31): $4—$150. Similarly valuable for his OKE, VOC, AUT, BRN sides before 1928.

OLSEN, George	NMV. Symbolic of the Roaring 20's. Lost his growl in the 30's.
ORIGINAL MEMPHIS FIVE*	Group made music for many labels. Look for: GEN, VOC, PAR, PAT, VIC, BRN particularly (1919-29). Zone: $3—$6.
OSBORNE, Will	NMV. Nice voice, sliding trombones, four dimes.
OWENS, Harry	NMV. No one's wild about Harry.
PASTOR, Tony	NMV. After he left Shaw, very little of value transpired on BLB.
PEERLESS QUARTET	NMV. Only the fearless blow a dime on Peerless.
PIED PIPERS	NMV. *Dream* on CAP is worth $1.50.
POLLACK, Ben*	Goodman, Miller, Bauduc, Teagarden, Matlock and other notables are on his VIC sides in the 20400-22270 range. All-stars also on BAN (32000 series); COL (2800-2900); BRN (7700 series).Deserving of respectful pricing at $5.
POWELL, Teddy	NMV for his underrated BLB orchestra.
PRIMA, Louis*	Good jazz on his BRN 7000 series (1934-36). Less significance as he moved to VOC, DEC, VAR in late 30's. Overall, a solid $3.50.
RAINEY, Ma*	On PAR exclusively (1923-28), Ma's records come in from $5—$15.
RAVAZZA, Carl	NMV. Tempest in a tearoom. Twenty cents a bag.
REDHEADS*	Red Nichols, of course, 1925-27 on COL, PER. Valued at $6.

REDMAN, Don*   Redman's 1931-34 BRN 6000's nearly rank
                        (musically) with Fletcher Henderson's efforts.
                        Excellent arrangements, solid Big Band jazz.
                        Try to bring him in at the $2.75—$3.50
                        range. He deserves it.

RED ONION   Very scarce item on GEN (1924). Armstrong
   JAZZ BABIES*   and friends: $40.

REICHMAN, Joe   NMV. Oh, Pagliacci.

REISMAN, Leo   NMV. Leo went out like a lamb in the 30's.

RENARD, Jacques   NMV. Fifty million Americans can't be
                        wrong. One quarter.

REVELERS   NMV. Pay someone to cart them off.

REY, Alvino   NMV. Perhaps $1.50 for his better BLB
                        records.

ROBESON, Paul   NMV so far. Maybe he will be fully appre-
                        ciated, someday. His VIC records should be
                        marked at $1, at least. Possible UPS.

RODGERS, Jimmie*   Rare, desirable, significant country-western
                        discs by Rodgers on VIC (1928-33) are valued
                        highly by special collectors. *Blue Yodel No. 9*
                        (VIC 23580) features Louis and Lil Armstrong.
                        $5—$15.

ROLFE, B.A.   NMV. Highly respected by colleagues in 20's.
                        No market today.

ROLLINI, Adrian   Early discs (1933-38) on BRN, BAN, VOC,
                        VIC, DEC warrant $1.50.

ROSS, Lanny   NMV. Faded moonlight and roses.

ROYAL HAWAIIAN   NMV. Three pennies per member.
   TRIO

RUSSELL, Andy   NMV. Tried hard on CAP. No action for this
                        melodic singer.

RUSSELL, Luis*	Keep eye peeled for VOC, OKE, BAN, VIC sides (1926-34) by Luis and star sidemen. Not common. Average tag: $6.
SAVITT, Jan	NMV. Some of his BLB, DEC, VIC hits might hover at $1.25.
SCOTT, Raymond	NMV. Coy, anecdotal arrangements. Very few recall his work.
SELVIN, Ben	NMV. Made more records than anyone, ever, on scores of labels. So diffused no one could concentrate on him. Sorry, Ben.
SHAND, Terry	NMV. Be a pirate and take 50 cents.
SHAW, Artie*	Shaw's BRN, VOC releases (1936-37) are uncommon; BLB, VIC discs less so, but still attractive. All in all, $1.50—$5.
SHERWOOD, Bobby	NMV. The Elks' parade is over.
SHILKRET, Nathaniel	NMV. He surfaces on VIC frequently. Submerge him for 50 cents.
SHORE, Dinah	NMV for COL discs. Early BLB, VIC hits tops at $1.50.
SIMEON, Omer*	Clarinetist on BRN 7000 series (1929), very scarce. Vicinity $7.
SIMMS, Ginny	NMV with or without Sully Mason and Harry Babbitt.
SINATRA, Frank	NMV. Market glutted with LPs. Up to $1 on a good day.
SISSLE, Noble*	Early EMR, PAR, Edison, VIC discs of 10 featured famous Eubie Blake, Sidney Bechet with Noble on BRN, DEC (1934-37). $4.
SLACK, Freddie	NMV. *Beat Me Daddy* Slack is beat.
SMITH, Bessie*	Great singer on COL (1923-33), VOC (1933). Range: $4—$10.

SMITH, Clara*   On COL (1923-29) with Bessie Smith, Armstrong, J.P. Johnson: $2.50—$7. Also accompanied by F. Henderson in 1923.

SMITH, Hazel*   On OKE (1928) accompanied by King Oliver, Clarence Williams: $12.

SMITH, Jabbo*   On BRN 7000 series (1929), his Rhythm Aces are valued at $25.

SMITH, Jack   NMV, for both smiling Jacks.

SMITH, Joseph C.   NMV. Frigid VIC orchestra of the 20's.

SMITH, Kate   NMV, but thawing out. Possible $1.50 for her classics.

SMITH, Trixie*   On BSW with J.P. Johnson and own group (1921-23); on her own and with Blythe's Ragamuffins on PAR (1924-26). Range: $5—$40, PAR: $8—$25.

SPANIER, Muggsy   Modest, well-deserved interest in his BLB discs (1939-40). $2.

SPECHT, Paul   His 1923-30 COL discs do not excite, but worth $1.75, historically.

SPITALNY, Phil   NMV. The magic in Evelyn's violin is long gone.

SPIVAK, Charlie   NMV. Squeeze off $1.50 for *Stardreams; Let's Go Home* on OKE.

STAFFORD, Jo   NMV for CAP records. Vibrating at 50-cent level.

STATE STREET   Personnel varies on GEN, CHA between
RAMBLERS*   1927-31. All good at $15.

TEAGARDEN, Jack*   Steady affection for Big T's work has not translated into big market. 1930-34 on BAN, PER, COL, BRN perhaps $2—$3. Down to $1.50 for 1938-41 efforts on BRN, COL, OKE.

THOMAS, Hersal*   1925-26 on OKE with Sippie Wallace and others: $6—$40.

THORNHILL, Claude   NMV unfortunately. OKE, COL discs go for $1, maximum.

TRACE, Al   NMV. Beg someone to pay 50 cents for *Mairzy Doats*.

TRAVELERS*   The Dorseys and others on OKE (1929): $4.

TROUBADOURS   NMV. Their VIC discs (1923-31) just will not go away.

TRUMBAUER, Frankie*   His OKE discs (1927-28) feature Bix, Rollini, Venuti, other stars; 1929-36 sessions for OKE, BRN, VIC, COL less spectacular. Zone: $3—$15.

TUCKER, Tommy   NMV. *I Don't Want to Set the World on Fire*, other hits: $1.25.

VALLEE, Rudy   NMV. Possible $1.25 for famous vocals.

VENUTI, Joe*   Significant figure in jazz-pop history. Many labels: COL, OKE, VIC, VOC, MEL, PER, starting 1926. PER: $4; OKE: $3—$8.

VICTOR ORCHESTRAS   NMV. Whether it be called "dance," "concert," or "salon"—no sale.

VIRGINIANS   Fair low-key jazz group on VIC (1923-28). Hard to say more than $1.

WALLACE, Sippie*   On OKE with Clarence Williams (1924), Perry Bradford (1925), Armstrong (1926-27), Hersal Thomas (1925), and on VIC (1929). Zone: $4—$30.

WALLER, Fats*   On VIC mainly (1926-42). Early works should be set in the $2—$8 range. Back off to $1.50—$2 for 1938-42 discs. Great favorite.

WARING, Fred   NMV. Sleep, Sleep, Sleep on VIC, DEC.

WARNOW, Mark	NMV. Hit Parade orchestra ran out of hits.
WATERS, Ethel*	Range: $6—$12 for vocals on BSW, COL, PAR, BRN. Scarce.
WEBB, Chick	Many fans, but NMV. Possible $1.50 for sides with Ella Fitzgerald.
WEEMS, Ted	NMV. $1.25 top for his big hits, and sides featuring Perry Como on DEC.
WELK, Lawrence	NMV. Not so "wunnerful" in 30's and 40's, but if you come across his hotsy-totsy 1928 sides for GEN you might assess them at $2.75.
WHITEMAN, Paul*	NMV with these possible exceptions: 1927-28 VIC series (21100-21400) which feature Bix, Dorseys, Busse, Bing Crosby; 1928-29 COL 1400 and 50000 series with Bix, Crosby, Trumbauer. For these, $2—$4.
WHITING, Margaret	NMV. *Moonlight in Vermont/My Ideal* on CAP potential $1.
WILLIAMS, Clarence*	On OKE (1923-28): $3—$50; QRS (1928): $7—$20.
WILSON, Teddy*	BRN discs made between 1935-39 move from $2—$6.
WOLVERINES*	On GEN (1924) with Bix primarily: $35. Several other groups by same name in 20's, not worth as much.

Part Eight

Remembrance: A Necrology

Rembrance: A Necrology

A selective bow to deceased artists, many of whom reside comfortably in the imaginations of those of us who grew up during the halcyon years (1918-48) of popular 78 rpm record.

Irving Aaronson (1895-1963)

Bert Ambrose (1897-1971)

Ivie Anderson (1904-1949)

Louis Armstrong (1900-1971)

Gus Arnheim (1897-1955)

Mitchell Ayres (1910-1969)

Bix Beiderbecke (1903-1931)

Bunny Berigan (1909-1942)

Ben Bernie (1891-1943)

Don Bestor (1889-1970)

Earl Bostic (1913-1965)

Al Bowlly (1898-1941)

Tiny Bradshaw (1905-1969)

Henry Busse (1894-1955)

Buddy Clark (1912-1949)

Nat "King" Cole (1919-1965)

Zez Confrey (1895-1972)

Charlie Cook (1891-1956)

Carleton Coon (1894-1932)

Frank Dailey (1901-1956)

Eddie DeLange (1904-1949)

Jack Denny (1894-1950)

Carroll Dickerson (1895-1957)

Sam Donahue (1918-1974)

Jimmy Dorsey (1904-1957)

Tommy Dorsey (1905-1956)

Eddy Duchin (1909-1951)

Duke Ellington (1899-1974)

Skinnay Ennis (1909-1963)

Jim Europe (1881-1919)

Jean Goldkette (1899-1962)

Glen Gray (1906-1963)

W.C. Handy (1873-1958)

Coleman Hawkins (1904-1969)

Ted Heath (1902-1969)

Fletcher Henderson (1898-1952)

Art Hickman (1886-1930)

Tiny Hill (1906-1972)

Richard Himber (1907-1966)

Les Hite (1903-1962)

Johnny Hodges (1906-1970)

Eddy Howard (1914-1963)

Jack Jenney (1910-1945)

Isham Jones (1894-1956)

Spike Jones (1911-1965)

Roger Wolfe Kahn (1907-1962)

Art Kassel (1896-1965)

Hal Kemp (1905-1940)

Freddie Keppard (1889-1933)

Gene Krupa (1909-1963)

Ted Lewis (1892-1971)

Johnny Long (1916-1972)

Vincent Lopez (1898-1975)

Bert Lown (1903-1962)

Jimmie Lunceford (1902-1947)

Fate Marable (1890-1947)

Abe Lyman (1897-1957)

Johnny Marvin (1897-1944)

Hal McIntyre (1914-1959)

Glenn Miller (1904-1944)

Lucky Millinder (1900-1966)

Vaughn Monroe (1911-1973)

Russ Morgan (1904-1969)

Bennie Moten (1894-1935)

Ozzie Nelson (1906-1975)

Red Nichols (1905-1965)

Phil Ohman (1896-1954)

King Oliver (1895-1938)

George Olsen (1903-1971)

Oran Page (1908-1954)

Tony Pastor (1907-1969)

Ben Pollack (1903-1971)

Boyd Raeburn (1913-1966)

Don Redman (1900-1963)

Joe Reichman (1898-1970)

Leo Reisman (1897-1961)

B.A. Rolfe (1879-1956)

Jimmy Rushing (1903-1972)

Luis Russell (1902-1963)

Joe Sanders (1896-1965)

Kenny Sargent (1906-1969)

Jan Savitt (1913-1948)

Noble Sissle (1889-1975)

Freddie Slack (1910-1965)

Muggsy Spanier (1906-1967)

Paul Specht (1895-1954)

Phil Spitalny (1890-1970)

Jack Teagarden (1905-1964)

Claude Thornhill (1909-1965)

Alphonso Trent (1905-1959)

Jerry Wald (1918-1973)

Fats Waller (1904-1943)

Chick Webb (1907-1939)

Anson Weeks (1896-1969)

Ted Weems (1901-1963)

Paul Whiteman (1890-1967)

Bob Zurke (1912-1944)

Part Nine

Sources for Further Reading

Sources for Further Reading

Rudi Blesh, *Eight Lives in Jazz, Combo: USA* (New York, 1971).

David E. Cooper, *International Bibliography of Discographies* (Littleton, Colorado, 1975).

Charles Delauney, *New Hot Discography* (New York, 1948).

Leonard Feather, *The New Encyclopedia of Jazz* (New York 1962).

Gene Fernett, *Swing Out: Great Negro Dance Bands* (Michigan, 1970).

John Flower, *Moonlight Serenade: A Bio-Discography of the Glenn Miller Civilian Band* (New York, 1972).

Roland Gelatt, *The Fabulous Phonograph* (New York, 1955).

Charles Hager, *When Was That Old Record Made?* (Dallas, 1973).

Orrin Keepnews and Bill Grauer, Jr., *A Pictorial History of Jazz* (New York, 1957).

Roger D. Kinkle, *The Complete Encyclopedia of Popular Music and Jazz* (New Rochelle, 1974), 4 vols.

Irving Kolodin and Benny Goodman, *The Kingdom of Swing* (New York, 1939).

Neil Leonard, *Jazz and the White Americans* (Chicago, 1962).

Albert J. McCarthy, *The Dance Band Era* (Philadelphia, 1971).

Idem, *Big Band Jazz* (New York, 1974).

Julian M. Moses, ed., *Price Guide to Collectors' Records* (New York, 1967).

Joseph Murrells, *Daily Mail Book of Golden Discs: 1903-65* (London, 1966).

Brian Rust, *Jazz Records: 1897-1942* (London, 1972), 2 vols.

Herb Sanford, *Tommy and Jimmy: The Dorsey Years* (New Rochelle, 1972).

George T. Simon, *The Big Bands* (New York, 1967).

Idem, *Glenn Miller and His Orchestra* (New York, 1974).

Peter A. Soderbergh, "Moonlight and Shadows: The Big Bands, 1934-1974," *Midwest Quarterly*, XVI (Autumn, 1974), pp. 85-96.

Idem, "Just an Old Fashioned Love Song?," *American Collector* (May, 1975), pp. 10-11.

Leo Walker, *The Wonderful Era of the Great Dance Bands* (New York, 1972).

Frederick P. Williams: "Ideas On Beginning A 78's Record Collection," (Phildelphia, 1973), pp. 49.